A PRACTICAL GUIDE
TO THE TREATMENT
OF BULIMIA NERVOSA

BRUNNER/MAZEL
EATING DISORDERS MONOGRAPH SERIES

Series Editors
PAUL E. GARFINKEL, M.D.
DAVID M. GARNER, PH.D.

BRUNNER/MAZEL EATING DISORDERS MONOGRAPH SERIES NO. 6

A PRACTICAL GUIDE TO THE TREATMENT OF BULIMIA NERVOSA

JOHAN VANDERLINDEN, PH.D.

JAN NORRÉ, M.A.

WALTER VANDEREYCKEN, M.D., PH.D.

BRUNNER/MAZEL, *Publishers* • New York

Library of Congress Cataloging-in-Publication Data
Vanderlinden, Johan.
    [Behandeling van boulime. English]
    A practical guide to the treatment of bulimia nervosa / Johan
Vanderlinden, Jan Norré, and Walter Vandereycken.
      p. cm. — (Brunner/Mazel eating disorders monograph series ;
no. 6)
    Translation of: De behandeling van boulimie. c1989.
    Includes bibliographical references and index.
    ISBN 0-87630-656-3
    1. Bulimia—Treatment. I. Norré, Jan. II. Vandereycken, Walter,
III. Title. IV. Series: Brunner/Mazel eating disorders
monograph series ; 6.
    [DNLM: 1. Bulimia—therapy. W1 BR917D v. 6 / WM 175 V235b]
RD552.B84V36 1992
    616.85'263—dc20
DNLM/DLC
for Library of Congress   91-40876
                                                          CIP

Originally published as *De Behandeling van Boulimie:*
Een Gids Voor de Therapeutische Praktij
Copyright 1989, Vanderlinden, Norré, and Vandereycken

Copyright © 1992 by Brunner/Mazel, Inc.

All rights reserved. No part of this book may be
reproduced by any process whatsoever without
the written permission of the copyright owner.

Published by
BRUNNER/MAZEL, INC.
19 Union Square West
New York, New York 10003

Manufactured in the United States of America

10 9 8 7 6 5 4 3 2 1

Contents

About the Authors

Johan Vanderlinden, Ph.D., is a Clinical Psychologist working in the Eating Disorders Unit of the University Center St.-Jozef, Kortenberg, Belgium. He is also the coauthor of two books and several articles on both the research and therapy of eating disorders.

Jan Norré, M.A., is a Clinical Psychologist working in private practice. He is also consulting psychologist to the Center for Fertility Research and Treatment, Leuven, Belgium.

Walter Vandereycken, M.D., Ph.D., is Professor of Psychiatry at the University of Leuven. He is Clinical Director of the Department of Behavior Therapy at the Alexian Brothers Psychiatric Hospital in Tienen and Consultant Psychiatrist to the Eating Disorders Unit of the University Center St.-Jozef, Kortenberg, Belgium.

Preface

The specific aim of this book is to present a wide variety of therapeutic methods and strategies to a large audience of professionals (psychiatrists and other physicians, psychologists, nurses, social workers, occupational therapists, dieticians, and counselors) working with bulimia nervosa (BN) patients.* We will not present innovative theories or impressive research data, nor engage ourselves in academic discussions. This practice-oriented book is devoted to the description of a variety of therapeutic strategies for both outpatients and inpatients. Our approach can be characterized as directive and eclectic, using a flexible framework that is governed by everyday pragmatism instead of orthodox ideology.

This book reflects the extensive clinical experience and research of a multidisciplinary team. Since we consider bulimia nervosa a multidetermined problem, the reader will quickly ascertain that we recommend a directive and multidimensional treatment, integrating strategies from different therapeutic models. Our approach will be demonstrated in individual, group, and family therapy. Our emphasis is always on clinical practice, including failures. Hence we offer neither encyclopedia nor cookbook, but a pragmatic guide for the critical practitioner.

---

*Bulimia nervosa is abbreviated as BN. Since we are male therapists and almost exclusively treat female patients, these are the gender distinctions we use throughout the text.

Chapter 1 describes the problems in detecting and diagnosing BN. It stresses the need for accurate differential diagnosis and also discusses somatic aspects.

Chapter 2 critically analyzes the various assumptions and therapeutic models that have been proposed for BN. We promote a multidimensional, pragmatic, and eclectic approach, combining various models.

The multidimensional assessment and treatment planning of BN are addressed in Chapter 3. The bulimic symptoms are assessed on different levels, using various methods. Indications for pharmacotherapy and inpatient versus outpatient treatment are outlined. Guidelines to start treatment—based on a detailed functional analysis—are described.

Chapter 4 presents an individual cognitive-behavioral approach on an outpatient basis. Starting with a detailed functional analysis and assessment of the patient's motivation, different techniques to regain self-control over the eating behavior and the bingeing-vomiting cycle are demonstrated with an extensive case example.

The general characteristics of our group approach are presented first in Chapter 5, and then specific therapeutic strategies for the different phases in the treatment process are described. These are illustrated with a detailed case example.

Chapter 6 describes how hypnotherapeutic techniques can be integrated in a multidimensional approach as demonstrated with an extensive case example.

In Chapter 7 our family therapeutic approach is presented. Specific therapeutic techniques and strategies appropriate to the different treatment phases are described, together with some special interventions and possible pitfalls in family therapy with BN. Another case example will illustrate these issues.

The basic guidelines of our inpatient treatment program for BN are summarized in Chapter 8. The treatment contract and the various group-oriented therapeutic activities are briefly presented.

Chapter 9 critically addresses the issue of treatment evaluation and will close with the classic observation that "more research is needed," especially with regard to differential treatment effects and prognostic factors.

Acknowledgments

We would like to thank Arnout Meeussen and Pascale Geirnaert for their invaluable help in the preparation of this book. Although it is but one form of getting rid of our guilt feelings, we are most grateful to our wives and children for having accepted our "bulimic" time consumption while writing this book.

1

Diagnosis

DETECTION

Bulimia can be described as an irresistible urge for usually very calorie-rich food, which manifests itself in periods of overeating during which the subject experiences loss of control over the eating behavior. This overeating is followed by vomiting (usually self-induced), abuse of laxatives and/or diuretics, or rigorous fasting in order for the subject to keep his or her weight under control for fear of becoming fat. The precise definition of the essential diagnostic criteria has kicked up quite a lot of scientific dust (see Garner & Garfinkel, 1988). There are several causes for the confusion in the literature:

1. The failure to make a distinction between bulimia as a symptom and as a syndrome or otherwise (Vandereycken & Meermann, 1984)
2. The occurrence of bulimia in anorexia nervosa and obese patients, as well as in a growing number of women with a normal weight
3. Large individual differences in response to treatment
4. The complexity of the disturbed behavior, due to the interaction of social, psychological, and biological factors (Garner, Rockert, Olmsted, Johnson, & Coscina, 1985)

In order to prevent misunderstandings we shall make in this book a clear distinction between bulimia as a symptom and as a syndrome.

Bulimia as a Symptom

Bulimia as a symptom or separate dysfunctional component of behavior (synonyms: hyperorexia, compulsive eating, binge eating) refers to an uncontrollable urge to eat large quantities of food. This can be linked to various forms of mental disorders and organic pathology (e.g., brain tumors). To be complete, we mention the following variants of bulimia that are not directly considered to be problematic:

- Situational bulimia, which is of frequent occurrence in student societies but without serious consequences
- Stress-reducing bulimia without fear of becoming fat
- Hedonic bulimia or pleasantly experienced bingeing episodes without fear of becoming fat and not followed by vomiting or abuse of pills

There also exist forms of psychogenic vomiting without eating problems: These occur either chronically or episodically in patients who are not concerned about their weight.

Bulimia as a Syndrome

Bulimia as a syndrome has been described under various denominations: bulimia, bulimia nervosa, bulimarexia, bulimic syndrome, hyperorexia nervosa, thin-fat syndrome, dietary chaos syndrome, abnormal normal weight control syndrome, stuffing syndrome, compulsive eating, night eating syndrome, gorging-purging syndrome. Russell (1979) was the first to mark out the diagnostic criteria of this syndrome and named it "bulimia nervosa" (BN) in order to underline the relationship with anorexia nervosa. The much broader description of "bulimia" in the third edition of the *Diagnostic and Statistical Manual of Mental Disorders* (DSM-III) (1980) provoked a flood of critical reactions (Fairburn & Garner,

1986) and finally led to a few profound alterations in the revised third edition, DSM-III-R (1987), which can be labeled as considerable progress:

- It is now called "bulimia nervosa" (Russell's description) in order to avoid terminological confusion with bulimia as a symptom and to underline the narrow link with anorexia nervosa.
- The essential characteristics of the syndrome are mentioned explicitly: episodes of binge eating as an expression of the experienced loss of control, use of various methods of weight control, and morbid preoccupation with body size and weight.
- There is now an index (be it arbitrary) denoting the degree of gravity.

BN therefore implies more than just episodes of binge eating. The diagnosis requires the five characteristics indicated in Table 1. This enables us to mark out BN against bulimia or binge eating as a symptom.

BN can now be described as a regularly occurring *loss of control* over the eating behavior, resulting in frequent episodes of

---

TABLE 1
Diagnostic Criteria for Bulimia Nervosa
(according to DSM-III-R)

A. Repeated episodes of rapid consumption of large amounts of food (binge eating).
B. A feeling of loss of control over eating behavior during binge eating.
C. In order to prevent weight gain, the subject regularly engages in either self-induced vomiting, strict dieting or fasting, the use of laxatives or diuretics, or vigorous physical exercise.
D. A minimum of two binge eating episodes per week for at least three months.
E. Persistent preoccupation with body shape and weight.

binge eating and a disturbed eating pattern. These binges are followed by vomiting (usually self-induced), abuse of laxatives and/or diuretics, rigorous fasting, or hyperactivity in order to prevent weight gain. A variant to this is the "chewing-spitting syndrome": The subject eats very slowly, lets the food melt in the mouth, and then spits it out (Vandereycken & Meermann, 1984).

Though the body weight usually falls within the normal limits, there is a *morbid preoccupation with body shape and weight*. The central point is fear of loss of control over the eating behavior and resulting increase in weight. The patient is aware of the abnormal character of this eating behavior, and the periods of binge eating are often followed by depressive feelings and thoughts (shame and guilt), though these are not essential for the diagnosis (Fairburn & Garner, 1986; Fairburn, 1987). Most salient is the bingeing-vomiting cycle. In practice, a large diversity is to be found. Yet, on the basis of the most important characteristics, we can typify this disturbed eating pattern as follows:

1. Usual periods of binge eating comprise the excessive absorption of mostly calorie-rich food (varying from 1,000 to 10,000 calories and sometimes more). The more distinct the neutralization strategies are (particularly vomiting and/or purging), the more disturbed the eating pattern goes off. The excessiveness lies rather in the subjective experience than in the quantity: Some patients regard the absorption of even small quantities of "forbidden" food as a binge; others are not satisfied with vomiting and also use appetite suppressants, laxatives, and diuretics.

2. Patients experience an uncontrollable urge to eat and/or fear of being unable to stop eating as soon as they have started. It looks like a self-alienated (ego-dystonic) force that they cannot resist.

3. The period of binge eating occurs when one is by oneself, mostly in secret, at any time of the day, but often after work or school, in the evening or even at night. Some have so strong an urge, that they take no notice of the presence of others.

4. The emotional state just before a binge eating can be described as a particular form of inner anxiety or tenseness. The periods of binge eating can be induced by:

   • A feeling of hunger
   • The desire to eat "forbidden" food
   • Certain negative emotional states such as anxiety, sadness, anger, or disappointment (for instance, because of increase in weight), boredom, and loneliness

5. The frequency varies very strongly, but as a whole one can assume that half of the patients have at least one period of binge eating per day.

6. A period of binge eating varies considerably in duration, from a few minutes to several hours, and it often takes on a ritual character.

7. There is a typical food preference in a binge-eating episode:

   • Calorie-rich food (mostly sweet and fat), which is inconsistent with the diet the subject wishes to go on
   • Food that needs little preparation
   • Sometimes the same food always, but in exaggerated amounts

8. Often these binges or the opportunities to have them are planned in advance. However, at the moment itself the binge may have a paroxysmal character, as if it occurred suddenly and with an actual loss of control:

   • Subjects are hardly conscious of the action itself.
   • They eat mostly without any taste, though for some a

pleasant and tranquillizing aspect appears to be connected with it.

• They experience no feeling of satiation, and at the most an abdominal discomfort ("swollen" stomach, "stuffed" belly).

9. The binge is followed by the "aftermaths": Subjects feel swollen and uncomfortable; feelings of guilt and self-reproach stand out, for in spite of all good intentions or promises, they "let themselves go" once again.

10. The bingeing period is ended by:

• Going to sleep (tired, exhausted, a "rotten feeling," "forgetting about everything")
• "Purging" oneself, in order to prevent becoming fat (vomiting; abuse of laxatives and/or diuretics; long periods of fasting, possibly with the help of appetite inhibitors)

11. The daily eating pattern is irregular in frequency, quantity, quality, and/or time schedule: "normal" meals are skipped or are extremely frugal. Others eat "normally" at fixed meals, or even much, but vomit afterwards.

12. Patients are very preoccupied with food and body shape (especially fear of becoming fat). For that reason they weigh themselves frequently, often immediately after vomiting as a control for weight stability. They have a wrong perception of their body, whose size they tend to overestimate (Wilmuth, Leitenberg, Rosen, Fondacaro, & Gross, 1985; Birtchnell, Hart, & Lacey, 1986; Vander-eycken, 1990b).

The dieting-bingeing-purging cycle (Figure 1) is a self-maintaining circle. Fasting, vomiting, and/or purging eases the fear of an increase in weight, but the preoccupation with food, body shape, and weight remains unchanged. In the beginning vomiting and abuse of laxatives are often experienced as a sign of control after periods of excessive food intake. Still, in the long term these practices result in ever-increasing loss of self-control; they "legitimate" the vomiting to such an extent that one feels one has to throw up everything one eats. Central in this cycle is the morbid fear of becoming fat ("weight phobia"), an essential characteristic that these patients have in common with anorexia nervosa patients.

Many misconceptions about the effectiveness of methods for weight control exist in the patients. Vomiting fails in the elimi-

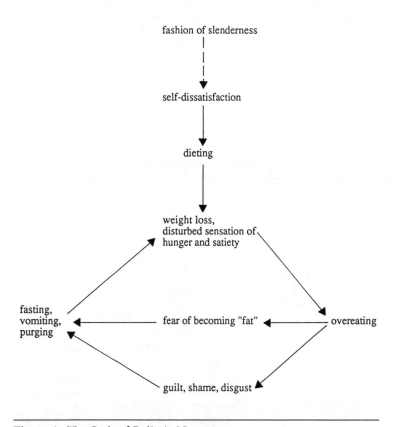

Figure 1. The Cycle of Bulimia Nervosa.

nation of all calories from the stomach, even to such an extent that frequently occurring cycles may still lead to weight gain. Laxatives work to empty the intestinal system after the calories have already been largely absorbed. The misconception is based on the experience that a quick weight loss can occur: this, however, is largely loss of fluid, followed by water retention, to result again in increase of weight. A similar situation arises with the intake of diuretics, which have absolutely no effect on the consumption of calories. These behaviors have a radical effect on health, as summarized in Table 2 (Garner et al., 1985; Mitchell, Hutsukami, Goff, Pyle, Echert, & Davis, 1985b; Vandereycken & Meermann, 1984). One of the most important damaging consequences is the disturbed electrolytes balance, namely, hypokalemia-alkalosis, which may cause highly dangerous heart rhythm disorders.

TABLE 2
Medical Complications

Bingeing	Vomiting	Laxative abuse
Acute stomach dilatation and risk of stomach rupture	Metabolic disorders (hypokalemia alkalosis)	
Menstrual disorder (irregular or absent)	Heart rhythm disorders	
Endocrinologic disorders	Tetany	
Painless swelling of salivary glands	Lethargy	
	Dehydration	
	Epileptic seizures	
	Renal damage	
	Dental decay (enamel injury)	Diarrhea
		Edemas
	Chronic hoarseness and sore throat	Drumstick fingers
	Gastrointestinal reflex and esophagitis	

DIFFERENTIAL DIAGNOSIS

Besides the essential characteristics of BN, we now discuss associated psychopathology, which is not essential for the diagnosis. However, this psychopathology creates several subgroups of BN patients. And there is growing evidence that this differentiation could be relevant to the treatment plan.

In the first place, BN patients experience symptoms of *depression* such as sadness, sleep disorders, concentration problems, fatigue, pessimistic thoughts, suicidal tendencies, and low self-esteem (Fairburn, 1985; Mitchell & Pyle, 1992; Rosen & Leitenberg, 1988). This has led to the examination of the relationship between BN and mood disorders (see Chapter 2).

Other problems are *impulsiveness and addictions* (Andersen, 1985; Lacey, 1986; Mitchell & Pyle, 1992). This is best illustrated by the way in which the binge itself takes place. The disturbed eating pattern can lead to serious financial difficulties, which induces some patients to steal money or food to satisfy this urge. Abuse of (or addiction to) alcohol, medicines, and drugs is also reported, and some patients show promiscuous behavior. Sometimes self-mutilation also occurs. These observations raised the question as to whether BN could be considered as a form of addiction (an urge for food or sweets). This question will be analyzed in Chapter 2.

A general observation is that BN patients maintain an *obsessional* or *perfectionist attitude*, accompanied by all-or-none reasoning (Knight & Litton, 1984; Polivy & Herman, 1985). This black-and-white attitude is already expressed in the eating pattern: Once the "forbidden fruit" has been tasted, all diet rules are thrown overboard and the patient breaks into a "gallop" (binge), because the diet is "messed up anyway." On the other hand, a black-and-white attitude is also observed in the approach to other life situations, for instance, in difficulties with experiencing and/or expressing principally negative feelings: Anxiety, anger, frustration, or disappointment is either not recognized (repressed) for fear of loss of control or expressed without inhibition (actual loss of control).

The disturbed eating behavior also has a marked influence on *social relations* (Knight & Litton, 1984; Lacey, Cohen, & Birtchnell, 1986; Mitchell & Pyle, 1992). There are often difficulties in study or work: concentration problems because of the preoccupation with food and weight or because of lack of time or fatigue as a result of the bingeing-vomiting ritual. Because patients are ashamed of their eating behavior and afraid of being caught, they avoid more and more contacts with peers and family members. This loneliness enhances the feeling of being excluded and heightens their feelings of insufficiency, which in turn can lead to bingeing. Moreover, many show a lack of social skills, which makes them avoid unpleasant feelings or "expected" rejections in social relations. In heterosexual relations they maintain traditional sex role attitudes and experience little satisfaction in sexual contact (in spite of the sometimes licentious or even promiscuous behavior).

This observed psychopathologic behavior raises the question about the presence of *personality disorders* in eating disorders patients. Lacey (1985) spoke about a personality disorder group, in which manipulation of food is associated with drug, alcohol, and sex abuse. The clinical presentation of these patients was "histrionic." Wonderlich, Smitt, Slotnick, and Goodman (1990) found a significantly high rate of histrionic personality disorder in normal-weight bulimics. This supports the descriptions of the bulimic as being impulsive, interpersonally sensitive, affectively unstable, and driven to receive approval and affirmation. The borderline personality disorder is characterized by a loss of impulse control in several areas, a history of sexual abuse, self-destructiveness, and perceptions of hostility in parental relationships. But the prevalence of this personality disorder is the same in the different types of eating disorders. The personality disorders in normal-weight bulimics did not differ from those in bulimic anorexics or normal-weight bulimics with a history of anorexia nervosa (Wonderlich et al., 1990). The assessment of the personality disorder in BN patients may lead to several subtypes with important relevance for treatment selection and outcome (see Chapters 3 and 9).

In addition to their having possible common ground with a few psychiatric disorders, we also raise the question as to whether BN and *anorexia nervosa* are distinct clinical entities. The most striking similarity is the morbid fear of becoming fat and the pursuit of slenderness as a means to solve problems and/or deal with painful feelings. Both eating disorders are subject to the strong sociocultural influence of the slenderness ideal. This leads, especially in women, to preoccupation with food, weight, and diets. A close connection between both syndromes also appears based on the fact that, after a certain period of time, many anorexics develop bulimia and eventually even show the complete image of BN. Though the latter can be accompanied by periods of fasting, a BN patient seldom develops a complete and persistent anorexia nervosa. All this argues in favor of a dynamic and dimensional view of eating/weight problems: The clinical image of an eating disorder can after a long time undergo modifications and should not be considered as a static entity (Vandereycken & Meermann, 1984; Fairburn & Garner, 1986).

2

Treatment Models

To meet the increasing demand for help for BN patients, experiments have been made in recent years with different approaches and with different treatment programs. BN can be regarded as a symptom of an affective disorder, as a sign of lack of impulse control, as a conditioned response maintained by negative reinforcement, as a result of dysfunctional cognitions, as an expression of a dissociative state, as a signal of a pathological family system, or as a symptom of an imposed socialization process in women. These divergent conceptions obviously have radical implications for the choice of treatment.

THE DEPRESSION MODEL

Mood disturbances are quite common in eating disorders. The question is whether the eating disorder is part of a mood disorder or whether depression is secondary to BN. There are five sorts of findings on the basis of which a close connection between eating disorders and affective disorders can be assumed (Pope & Hudson, 1985):

1. *Phenomenology*: Depressive symptoms are frequently observed in eating disorder patients.
2. *Course of the illness*: After treatment of the eating disorder, depressive symptoms are frequently observed in the follow-up.

3. *Family history*: A more than fortuitous incidence of affective disorders is found in relatives of eating disorder patients.
4. *Biological tests*: Cortisol aberrations and positive dexamethasone suppression tests are frequently observed in these patients.
5. *Treatment results*: Antidepressants may have favorable results in eating disorders.

On the basis of these arguments, the use of antidepressants would lead to an improvement of both the depression and the disturbed eating behavior (see Chapter 3 for discussion). From a psychotherapeutic viewpoint, the depression theory is strongly disputed (Cooper & Fairburn, 1986; Wilson, Rossiter, Kliefield, & Lindholm, 1986; Garner, Olmsted, Davis, Rockert, Goldbloom, & Eagle, 1990). It appears from an accurate functional analysis of the disturbed eating behavior that the fluctuations in mood are secondary to the eating behavior. In other words, depression is the result rather than the cause of BN. Successful remission of the eating behavior leads in itself to a significant reduction of depression and other psychopathology (Laessle, Schweiger, Fichter, & Pirke, 1988). The fact that the use of antidepressants renders some effect was probably due to the vagueness of the DSM-III criteria (1980), by which BN could not be differentiated from an affective disorder. Moreover, it appears from psychobiological research that the endocrinologic and metabolic alterations, which are supposed to be typical of affective disorders, can also be the result of starvation and intermittent dieting. In short, the above-mentioned arguments to regard BN as an equivalent of depression are disputable on many grounds: They concern argumentations on the basis of alleged analogy, while the methodology of the investigations is often disputable (Laessle et al., 1988; Vandereycken, 1987a).

An association between BN and affective disorder—whatever the true nature may be—is expressed in a subgroup of BN patients (with or without previous anorexia nervosa history), and we can distinguish three forms of temporary connections:

1. The depressive mood follows the occurrence of a binge. This is consistent with the idea that mood disturbances are a result of a serious eating problem. The depression disappears when the control over the eating behavior increases.
2. The depressive mood precedes a binge. This means that the affective disorder can be regarded as primary in a subgroup of BN patients, at least on the time dimension. In addition, recent findings reflect the presence of at least two patient subgroups whose affective experience during the binge-purge episodes was quite different. The borderline subgroup was more depressed at the onset of the binge-purge episode than was the nonborderline subgroup. This could indicate that the primary function of the bulimic behavior for borderline bulimics is to mediate depression. However, this vision doesn't explain the function of bingeing and purging for the nonborderline group. Their response is more consistent with the anxiety model (Steinberg, Tobin, & Johnson, 1990).
3. Patients with a long illness history may show both previous forms, creating a vicious circle. It is then no longer possible to tell cause from consequence.

THE ADDICTION MODEL

Bulimia, or excessive intake of food, especially sweet, rich food, can be considered a form of addiction. This analogy is supported by the following observations (Bemis, 1985; Vandereycken, 1990a):

1. Various impulse control disorders and abuse of alcohol or drugs are observed in a good many BN patients.
2. Addictions in relatives of BN patients occur more frequently than in the normal population.

3. The personality profile of BN patients shows strong similarities to that of alcoholics or drug addicts.

4. BN corresponds to the following criteria for addictions:

   - Loss of control
   - Preoccupation with the substance
   - Use of the substance to be able to deal with stress and negative feelings
   - Concealment
   - Persistence of addiction in spite of the repugnant results

A weakened impulse control is observed in BN patients as a result of an uncontrollable field of tension between the urge to starve themselves and the physiological need for food (Heilbrun, Bloomfield, & Bloomfield, 1986). The focus in this model is on the periods of starvation (between binges), which are responsible for the following physical and psychological side effects (Wooley & Wooley, 1985; Garner et al., 1985):

- Increase of neuroticism (in marked weight loss)
- Harmed working capacity
- Strong preoccupation with food
- Urge for food as an uncontrollable reality
- Disturbances in the feeling of hunger and satiation

Another important result of starvation is the retardation of the metabolic processes as a compensatory reaction to the food deprivation. This explains one of the obstacles in the therapy: In the replacement of the fasting-bingeing cycle by a normal eating pattern, the patient is faced with a rapid but short increase in weight, which restores itself as soon as the metabolism functions normally. Two possible explanations might play a role herein: First, the body has to adapt itself to abnormal eating habits and, second, the patient eats mainly sweets during a binge and it is exactly the sugars that are absorbed before vomiting. When the body adapts itself to such a "sugar diet," this can give rise to an increased insulin concentration in the blood, which can provoke a feeling of hunger. Premature stopping of eating creates a state of hypoglycemia, which easily explains that the eating of one single cookie can give rise to an uncontrollable hunger. Research, however, indicates that there is no univocal connection between reactive hypoglycemia and BN (Hohlstein, Gwirtsman, Whalen, & Enns, 1986). We should, nevertheless, take into account that these physiological processes may play a role in the chronicity of the binge-purge episodes and that certain eating disorders may be connected with forms of diabetes.

According to another theory the conditioning process of the feeling of satiation is attached (Knapp, 1983). During a bingeing-vomiting cycle the body is constantly given erroneous information, so that the hunger is not checked unless enormous quantities are consumed. The stomach content increases progressively, so that an exceptional amount can be eaten before one is "stuffed."

A basic assumption is that restrained eating or fasting leads to bingeing (Polivy & Herman, 1985). This implies that periods of eating nothing or little must be stopped; in other words, it implies *acquiring a healthy and well-balanced eating pattern*, a principle that is central in most therapeutic programs (Fairburn, 1985; Lacey, 1985; Mitchell et al., 1985b; Wilson et al., 1986). A dietician's contribution may be meaningful, because the knowledge of BN patients about nutrition and energy consumption is insufficient. Patients must also cease to make a distinction between "good" and "bad" nourishment, and should eat varied meals. They should also become sensitive again to internal stimuli of hunger: the distinction between "mouth hunger" and "stomach hunger" (Orbach, 1978). Besides, the feeling of not being satiated persists in spite of their refraining from bingeing, and this goes on until the body is again metabolically adapted to "normal" nourishment.

The comparison of BN and addiction has given rise to the use of therapeutic techniques that have proved useful also in alcoholism and obesity, namely, *self-control and stimulus control techniques*. The most frequent self-control technique is the keeping of a structured diary (Fairburn, 1985; Lacey, 1985; Mitchell et al., 1985b; Wilson et al., 1986). This self-registration task forms the thread through the treatment and has a double purpose: The patient gains more insight into the disturbed eating pattern, and the therapist obtains interesting information to construct a functional analysis and plan therapeutic interventions. In the short run self-monitoring can lead to a temporary reduction of the symptoms, but it usually doesn't suffice by itself to influence the eating pattern in the long run.

Other self-control procedures follow:

- Planning meals at fixed places and preferably in the presence of others
- Temporary elimination of and subsequent progressive exposure to food-connected stimuli
- Introduction of alternatives when the urge for bingeing emerges (going for a walk, calling up a good friend, listening to music, etc.)
- Removing scales, diet books, and caloric lists
- Gradual delay of bingeing whenever the urge emerges and/or progressive response delay (extending the interval between bingeing and vomiting)

Mitchell et al. (1985b) have developed an intensive group-therapeutic program on the basis of the similarity between BN and addiction problems. This program of frequent evening sessions during 2 months is divided into three phases. During the first phase informatory lessons are given and group discussions held on subjects that are closely connected with BN: breaking through the chain of fasting-bingeing-vomiting, wholesome nourishment, depression, realistic planning, stress management, assertiveness training, self-management groups, rational-emotional techniques, relapse prevention. In the second phase there are exercises with techniques for promoting control over the eating behavior. Finally, in the third phase the individual development is discussed in group sessions. Research on the short-term outcome gave the following results: 47% reported no more bulimic episodes; 25%, about three per month; and 11%, five or more. There was also a significant improvement in psychosocial functioning: less depression, more social contacts, and a heightened self-esteem (Mitchell et al., 1985b). A follow-up 15 months later showed the same picture: a significant improvement without total abstinence (Mitchell, Davis, Goff, & Pyle, 1986). A third follow-up (Mitchell, Pyle, Eckert, Hatsukami, Pomeroy, & Zimmerman, 1988) 2 to 5 years later of 91 patients, of whom 79 (87%) had completed the intensive outpatient treatment program, was based on the self-reported eating behavior. Overall, 60 patients (66%) were doing well and reported freedom from bulimic episodes, although some had achieved remission through additional treatment, whereas 8 (9%) were improved but still symptomatic, and 23 (25%) were classified as treatment failures.

The advantages of a group-therapeutic approach in addiction inspired Brisman and Siegel (1985) to elaborate a "bulimia workshop," a weekend course to approach the addictive behavior in a directive way. The treatment starts with an intensive weekend program for the promotion of group cohesion, in which, on the basis of behavioral therapeutic principles, contracts are made to break and alter the symptomatic behavior. Difficulties are discussed in a follow-up session, and in a third phase (without a therapist) group members support one another in order to promote their own progress.

The analogy of BN to addiction raises the important question as to whether the bingeing-vomiting cycle should come to an end at once at the beginning of the treatment (*abstinence approach*) or whether a gradual reduction of the bulimic behavior should be aimed at, in which an improvement should not necessarily mean a complete absence of bulimic episodes (*nonabstinence approach*). Stopping the bulimic behavior gives the patient a feeling of personal control, enhances self-esteem, and offers the possibility of alternative problem-solving strategies. However, the clinical picture shows that even BN patients who at long-term follow-up are doing well have relapses during the recovery process; this indicates that the abstinence model is not the appropriate theoretical orientation (Mitchell & Pyle, in press). The nonabstinence approach states that the cognitive and emotional style in which BN patients approach life is both striking and disturbing (Bemis, 1985). When proceeding according to the abstinence model, the patients' absolutistic norms are enhanced and their abstinence behavior toward certain nutrients is cultivated. In the nonabstinence approach, the bulimic behavior remains the major treatment goal, but its alteration is only part of the global changing process. Thus, the overachievement attitude is undermined, and instead realistic goals are planned; special attention is paid to the prevention of relapses. A temporary relapse does not mean total failure. The bingeing-vomiting cycle is approached as something that can be brought under control. Besides, in the treatment of BN it concerns the extinction of a problematic behavior rather than the abstinence from a problematic substance (such as drugs and alcohol). So, the purpose is to learn to eat in a healthy way.

The analogy of addiction to bulimia is based on the statement of BN patients that they suffer from loss of control. We should ask ourselves whether this is a defense mechanism. Indeed, patients often describe their disorder as if they could not help it. But in doing so, they run away from their responsibility. In addition, the analogy does not hold because BN does not correspond to all essential characteristics of an addiction. The increasing absorption of food might indicate a certain tolerance or habituation, but most patients do not experience the stuffing as being at all pleasant, not to mention offering them any satisfaction. The only peak experience may lie in the vomiting, which is induced by the patient. We should rather ask ourselves whether BN patients are not rather "addicted" to dieting or restrained eating, in which a bulimic episode would be the breaking through of this dependence. If there would be a comparison with addiction, we presume that the crucial urge in bulimia would manifest itself in an extreme self-control over weight and body as it does in anorexia (Vandereycken, 1990a).

THE ANXIETY MODEL

This model draws an analogy between the anxiety-reducing effect of the vomiting (abuse of laxatives/diuretics, fasting) in BN and the compulsive hand washing or the repetitive control rituals in obsessive-compulsive disorders (Rosen & Leitenberg, 1988). Contrary to, for instance, a compulsive washer who avoids "dirt," the BN patient looks out for the provoking stimuli (the eating situation). Besides, positive consequences are connected to a binge-eating episode (eating pleasure; avoiding boredom, loneliness, sadness, anxiety, guilt, anger), but only and solely when the patient is certain to be able to vomit, which has a sedating function. Once this avoiding behavior is acquired, the vomiting becomes the driving force maintaining the continuance of binge eating. This model led to the use of exposure and response prevention techniques in the treatment of BN: The patient is faced with feared stimuli (for instance, calorie-rich food) or is induced to binge food, but the avoiding behavior (vomiting) is not allowed.

The rationale is that the binge episodes will gradually disappear if the patient acquires control over the vomiting. The kinds of food provoking anxiety are consumed in normal quantities according to a hierarchy of anxiety intensity during the therapy sessions. After the meal, the therapist draws the focus to the patient's anxiety-creating feelings and thoughts. Irrational thoughts about weight increase, bodily functions, nourishment, and the efficacy of vomiting are discussed via information and feedback. The therapy is effective only if vomiting does not occur within 2½ hours after each session, so that sufficient time elapses for digestion of the food; the patient can stay with the therapist until the urge to vomit is gone. As the therapy develops, patients learn to reformulate their problems as follows:

- The anxiety after eating "forbidden" food is less overwhelming than they feared.
- The consumption of normal meals does not automatically lead to any significant weight increase.
- Response prevention applied at home proves that patients have no binges if they resolve not to vomit.

It is more effective to apply this consistently 1 day in a week than to spread it over the week. Of course, the urge to be slender must be gradually reduced and made susceptible for discussion. The anxiety model has limited applicability for the following:

1. Patients in whom the link between eating behavior and self-induced vomiting is slight (for whom, for instance, no typical food provokes vomiting or provokes it only rarely)
2. Patients who vomit everything they eat
3. Patients who show no consistent bingeing-vomiting cycles

On the other hand, this approach can be a significant help to patients who do not succeed in constructing a regular eating pattern, (in particular, the integration of "forbidden" food into the meals) and patients who tend to vomit more than to binge.

The effectiveness of exposure and response prevention (or this combined with other cognitive or behavioral techniques) has not yet really been proved. In a controlled study evaluating the effectiveness of exposure plus response prevention in a sample of 47 women, Leitenberg, Rosen, Gross, Nudelman, and Vara (1988) concluded that this procedure in regard only to actual vomiting and eating behavior may add to the effects of a cognitive-behavioral approach. A replication study by Agras, Schneider, Arnow, Raeburn, and Telch (1989) didn't find any addition at all. Further research is needed to find out the clear indication criteria for the use of the exposure plus response prevention technique (Leitenberg & Rosen, 1989; Agras et al., 1989). This model is often used in a broader behavior therapy program (Giles, Young, & Young, 1985; Ordman & Kirschenbaum, 1985; Johnson, Schlundt, & Jarell, 1986; Wilson et al., 1986). One can expect results if vomiting is the driving force behind the disturbed eating behavior. But the theory is not sufficient to predict that the prevention of vomiting will lead to the extinction of the gorging behavior, because the latter can be directly reinforced by other positive and negative consequences. If exposure with response prevention is effective, we fail to know why. Cognitive and social learning theories postulate that the method is not based upon extinction of conditioned anxiety responses, but rather on the alteration of mediating cognitive processes (Wilson, 1989). Therapy increases the patient's sense of self-effectiveness, the experience of having one's own behavior under control again. This idea links up directly with the following model.

THE COGNITIVE MODEL

Central to this model is the idea that dysfunctional cognitions about food and weight, as well as a distorted body experience and inadequate problem-solving skills, play an essential role in the development and maintenance of BN. The most important cognitive dysfunction is the relentless pursuit of slenderness, which results in misconceptions and an exaggerated preoccupation with body shape, food, and weight. BN patients feel themselves "fatter" than they really are. Although this overestimation is not typical for eating disorder patients, it is very pronounced in BN and more distinct when the number of binges increases and the weight varies more from the normal (Freeman, Thomas, Solyom, & Koopman, 1985; Birtchnell et al., 1986). The ideas of BN patients about various diet practices are not only unrealistic, but often also unhealthy and based on a whole series of misconceptions about nutrition and weight control, such as the following:

- Eating normally, without vomiting, unconditionally gives cause to increase in weight.
- One calorie of protein-rich food is not the same as 1 calorie of sweets.
- Body weight must remain stable and should not fluctuate.

Their eating practices cause a disturbed internal perception of body stimuli: The feeling of hunger/satiation is distorted, the swelling of the stomach is experienced as threatening, and they can no longer enjoy eating. Nor are BN patients conscious of the risks of self-induced vomiting and abuse of laxatives/diuretics.

BN patients have a particular cognitive "style," characterized by a pronounced perfectionism and dichotomous thinking (Wilson, 1986; Thompson, Berg, & Shatford, 1987). Their eating behavior illustrates this vividly: "Either I keep my diet, or I forget about all the rules and I start bingeing." These patients are very self-exacting, which makes the realistic approach to problems and the pursuit of realistic goals often difficult, if not impossible. Hence, they suffer from manifest feelings of insufficiency, leading them to handle food as a coping mechanism in order to "benumb" themselves and get rid of negative feelings, run away from difficult situations, avoid boredom, and punish themselves. This increases their social isolation, and their involvement with food can assume such proportions that they structure the whole day's schedule around the bulimic ritual.

The implications of this cognitive model for therapy depend on the specific functional analysis of the problematic behavior. The cognitive behavioral program of Fairburn (1985) can be seen as a prototype of this model. This individual outpatient program comprises three phases. The first phase aims mainly at breaking through the disturbed eating pattern. The emphasis is on information and self-control. The therapist also makes contacts with important individuals from the immediate environment of the patient in order to obtain their cooperation. This phase seldom lasts longer than 8 weeks; there are two or three sessions per week. In the second phase the irrational cognitions and attitudes are accentuated. The eating pattern is stabilized and the patient should gradually give up dieting—that is, gradually incorporate the avoided food in the meals, and eventually eat everything. This forms an ideal opportunity to change certain conceptions about food and weight. The identification and alteration of these conceptions occur according to the well-known method of Beck for treating depressions. In addition, the patients are given training in problem solving. This phase lasts an average 8 weeks with weekly sessions. The third phase has a double purpose: First, the progress is further stabilized through the practicing of techniques of both preceding phases; second, the patient is prepared for problems that can occur in the future. This phase occupies three sessions, which take place once a fortnight.

The principles of this cognitive behavioral approach can be found in various therapeutic programs (Schneider & Agras, 1985; Kirkley, Schneider, Agras, & Bachman, 1985; Wilson, 1989; Hsu, 1990). However, not all programs attach the same importance to these dysfunctional cognitions. This depends on the causality model used by the therapist: Bingeing and vomiting can be regarded as an acquired habit, as a sign of repressed negative emotions, or as a form of loss of self-control and self-efficacy. As a function of the interpretation, cognitive restructuring plays a central role or is only one of the techniques in a broader treatment package.

Controlled studies have yielded results ranging from modest to highly positive. Freeman, Barry, Dunkeld-Turnbull, and Henderson (1988) found a structured behavioral approach as effective as a cognitive behavioral approach at the end of treatment and after a 1-year follow-up. Kirkley et al. (1985) found a cognitive-behavioral treatment more effective than a nondirective control treatment, but this superiority had disappeared at a 3-month follow-up. The most encouraging findings have been reported by Fairburn, Kirk, O'Connor, and Cooper (1986). The cognitive-behavioral therapy was superior to a short-term focal psychotherapy not in terms of its effects on the bulimic behavior, but in terms of its effects on patients' general clinical status, psychopathology, and social adjustment. Long-term follow-up research is not available.

THE DISSOCIATION MODEL

It was the famous French psychiatrist Pierre Janet who, at the turn of the century, first handled a dissociation model in the treatment of anorexia nervosa patients, but he also treated bulimic patients (Vanderlinden & Vandereycken, 1988c). An essential concept in Janet's theory is dissociation: A certain idea ("idée fixe"), or even a complex whole of conceptions with accompanying feelings, escapes the control and sometimes even the knowledge of personal consciousness. The escaped or dissociated idea starts living an independent life and urges the anorexic patient to refuse obstinately all food during the day, but, in the evening, to binge and afterward vomit uncontrollably. Such idées fixes have their origins, according to Janet, in a constitutional factor and violent emotions caused by some traumatic experience. On account of a constitutionally determined weakness, these patients begin to dissociate such traumatic experiences and feelings from their conscious mind.

Janet used hypnosis ("artificial somnabulism") to arouse this dissociated state, principally in hysterical patients who were particularly suggestible and therefore easily hypnotizable. Since Janet labeled most anorexics as hysterical, he often used hypnosis in this case to arouse a dissociated state and thus to detect the idée fixe underlying the eating disorder. In therapeutic practice Janet used, among others, a substitution technique to dissociate the idée fixe during hypnosis—for example, by altering certain parts of the idée fixe. To other patients, Janet first suggested they eat under hypnosis and gave posthypnotic suggestions that they would feel and behave normally after the session.

Janet's dissociation model for the the treatment of eating disorders fell into oblivion for more than half a century. This dissociation model was recently again advanced for the treatment of BN on account of both the enormous interest in bulimia and the revival of hypnosis. Various authors have recently emphasized the importance and possible influence of an ego-dissociation mechanism in the etiology and development of eating disorders (Torem, 1986a, 1986b, 1987; Barabasz, 1990). BN patients indeed often state that they switch into a different personality when bingeing and vomiting, as if they were possessed by the devil. Sometimes there even exists amnesia for what happened during the binge. For this reason various clinicians recently compared this phenomenon with a sort of dissociative experience. Torem (1986b, 1987) examined some 30 eating disorder patients and, in 12 of them, discovered dissociated ego states that were in disharmony with one another. He underlines the importance of the incorporation of hypnosis and hypnoanalytic explorative techniques as a routine part of the diagnosis of eating disorder patients. His treatment consists mainly of the identification of the dissociated ego state and the accomplishment of a negotiation between this ego state and the other part of the personality. The final objective is a better and more adequate integration of the dissociated ego state into the total personality.

This dissociation hypothesis in connection with the etiology of eating disorders seems to find some support in recent research findings (Pettinati, Horne, & Staats, 1985; Vanderlinden, Van Dyck, & Vandereycken, 1990). BN patients appear to be more hypnotizable than anorexics and a normal control group. Moreover, it has been indicated that the subgroup of purging anorexics show a higher score of hypnotizability than pure fasters. Another investigation (Sanders, 1986) concluded that students who binged regularly reported a higher degree of dissociation than those in the normal control group. These findings inspired us to test both the hypnotizability (using the Stanford Hypnotic Clinical Scale) and the presence of dissociation (using a new self-report questionnaire, the Dissociation Questionnaire or DIS-Q) in a group of 50 eating disorder patients (Vanderlinden et al., 1990). When comparing several subgroups, we found the highest scores on both hypnotizability and dissociation for the atypical eating disorder and bulimic group, significantly higher than the restricting anorexics, which confirms Pettinati and colleagues' findings (1985). There was a high correlation between the scores on the DIS-Q and hypnotizability. Because hypnosis, too, has been conceptualized as a dissociative process by many authors, it is suggested that bingeing and the ability to experience hypnosis may have a dissociative mechanism in common (see also Chapter 6).

THE FAMILY MODEL

The well-known systems theory approach of Minuchin, Rosman, and Baker (1978), who regard anorexia nervosa as a symptom of a dysfunctional family context, has contributed to the ever more frequent application of family therapy in eating disorders (Vandereycken, Kog, & Vanderlinden, 1989). The following characteristics are salient in families with BN patients:

1. They often belong to the higher social classes.
2. Eating disorders, somatic diseases, affective disorders, and addictions frequently occur in close relatives.
3. The family interactions are characterized by control and mutual emotional dependence, accompanied by strong ten-

sions and conflicts that are often not openly or directly expressed.

Investigations do not permit making causal connections, because it is not excluded that BN may cause disturbed family interactions instead of vice versa. This means that the occurrence of BN does not necessarily imply the presence of family pathology.

Much has been written about family therapy in anorexia nervosa, but little has been published on this approach with BN patients, presumably because the latter are often older, live alone, have a regular friend, or are married. The scarce literature is chiefly of a casuistic nature, and family therapy is mostly part of a broader treatment package. Yet a few important publications have appeared from a systems theoretical orientation. Schwartz, Barrett, and Saba (1985) developed an integrated approach in which specific attention is paid to the family interactions and individual measures are planned to regain control over the bulimic symptoms. These individual steps are necessary because, according to the authors, the symptoms continued to exist after restructuring of the family relationships. Their approach is based on complementary aspects of structural (Minuchin) and strategic (Haley, Selvini-Palazzoli) family therapy. They do not aim at the complete elimination of the binges, but rather at a change in the attitude of the patient toward food and weight, and parallel to this, changes in meaningful relations and patterns of thought. The treatment plan has three phases wherein individual sessions are alternated with family sessions. In the first phase, a context is created for change (themes within the family, resistance, symptom isolation, relabeling). The second phase is focused on abandoning the attitude of overprotection in the family and supporting the patient's independence, wherein also directives are given for the patient to gradually gain control of the binges. Finally, in the third phase special attention is paid to the continuation of changes. An interesting finding of these authors was that chronicity of the symptoms does not influence the results, and that there is less success in patients who continue to live at home (see Chapter 7).

In sharp contrast with the popularity of family therapy in eating disorders stands the almost complete neglect and absence of research concerning both outcome and process of the family therapy. Until now, only one controlled trial comparing family therapy with individual supportive therapy in anorexia nervosa and bulimia has been undertaken by Russell, Smukler, Dare, and Eisler (1987). Family therapy was found to be more effective than individual therapy in patients whose illness was not chronic and had begun before the age of 19 years. A more tentative finding was the greater value of individual supportive therapy in older patients.

In spite of the importance of the family context in BN, we believe that the restructuring of family relations is rarely sufficient to bring about long-term changes, not only in family functioning but also in the physical and psychosocial welfare of the patient as an autonomous individual. In order to attain these goals an intensive, multidimensional approach is required, in which the interactional context no doubt plays an important role. Family therapy can be one of the ingredients, but is no panacea. Moreover, a crisis in a family does not necessarily imply family pathology, and it may appear from a thorough assessment that there exists no disturbed family functioning at all (Vandereycken, 1987b).

THE FEMINIST MODEL

The broader sociocultural context of BN is the focus of the feminist model. For the last 20 years, a female slenderness ideal has been imposed in Western society as the magic clue to a happy and successful life. The pursuit of this slenderness ideal seems to take ever more unrealistic but also more destructive proportions. The advantages of slenderness are emphasized in an exaggerated way, whereas the disadvantages of being "overweight" are often exposed on unscientific grounds. The "ideal" shape of woman in the media has become thinner during the last two decades, whereas the body weight of the average adult woman in the Western world has increased. In order to bridge this increased discrepancy, the media continually unload diets, and fitness centers shoot up like mushrooms. Physical exercise ("fitness") becomes a new weapon in the struggle for control over the ideal weight. Moreover, much importance is attached to "looking young" in our society, which means that one should try to get rid of "superfluous fat." To crown it all, anorexia nervosa was uplifted to the status of "Golden Girls Disease"; and diets appear in fact to prescribe the symptoms of anorexia as the key to health and success. While some women devote themselves to the emancipation from traditional role patterns, others seem to submit themselves slavishly to the ruling slenderness ideal, which fits into the old pattern of "pleasing men."

The feminist model is based on the assumption that this social conditioning of women results in the repression of certain individual needs and aspects. The disturbed eating behavior symbolizes these underlying conflicts. In the approach of Orbach (1978) the focus of the group treatment is put on the awakening of the underlying intra- and interpersonal conflicts: A woman's relation to nourishment and to her body as well as the longing for dependence inhibit the recognition of her needs and desires. In the struggle for control of body weight, BN patients maintain the socially learned self-denial in order to be accepted as "good girls" by others. In the group-therapeutic approach of White and Boskind-Lodahl (1981), special attention is paid to the sociocultural significance of the disturbed eating behavior. They also make use of behavior therapeutic principles in order to teach BN patients some skills for a better control of the factors that provoke and maintain the disturbed eating behavior. A treatment model that lies on the boundary between the family model and the feminist model is the approach of Root, Fallon, and

Friedrich (1986). The theoretic assumptions of these therapists are the following:

1. The sex roles dictated by our society exert a destructive influence on both men and women.
2. The sociocultural context has a harmful impact on the family (from economical and political as well as juridical points of view) and often results in the phenomenon of the "overprotecting" mother and the "absent" father.
3. Most family problems are connected with problems about power and exceeding of boundaries in which men have greater social, economical, physical, and political power than women.
4. Many bulimics are victims of physical and sexual violence by men.

Root and colleagues (1986) very strongly recommend a family therapy, but radically reject a so-called neutrality of the therapist. The latter should, whenever confronted with women who are victims of physical and/or sexual violence, take a clear position and attribute the responsibility for this behavior completely to the male offender. Indeed, the feminist view accentuates a reality that can no longer be ignored—that is, the high incidence of unwanted sexual experiences, sexual abuse, and traumatic experiences in eating disorders patients reported upon recently (e.g., Hall, Tice, Beresford, Wooley, & Hall, 1989; Root & Fallon, 1989). But still a number of questions remain unanswered. In the first place, this view fails to give an adequate answer to the question how it is that certain women yield to this sociocultural pressure and develop an eating disorder, whereas others appear to have sufficient resistance. Besides, this model offers no explanation for the occurrence of eating disorders in men. There might be a real danger that the diagnosis of BN in males is not sufficiently recognized (Andersen, 1990).

THE ECLECTIC APPROACH

In the previous discussion of various models, it appears that the proposed treatment programs are often a matter of combining different forms of therapy. Few programs are a "pure" application of the theoretical model concerned. Many other therapeutic programs cannot be classified under one of the proposed models; they show rather an eclectic character. To illustrate this, we mention some of them.

Lacey (1985) suggests an eclectic approach on account of the heterogeneity of the bulimic population (he makes a distinction between those with secondary bulimia, a neurotic group, and a group with personality disorders, the so-called multi-impulsive BN). According to Lacey, on the one hand, there are inducing factors (relational difficulties, experiences of loss, and environmental changes), which should be approached in a group therapy that aims at giving insight (psychodynamic approach). On the other hand, there are maintaining factors (starving, stress, and loneliness): In individual sessions some structure is put into the chaotic eating pattern with the help of self-control and cognitive techniques (behavioral approach). The alternation of individual and group sessions is determined by the patients; the more they are prepared to realize that they can bring the symptoms under control, the more time they can devote to the group therapy aimed at giving insight. This short (10 weeks) program was quite successful in terms of its effects on the bulimic behavior as on the emotional problems, also at long-term follow-up with regular attendance at the treatment center (Lacey, 1985; 1992).

Wooley and Wooley (1985) and Wooley and Kearny-Cooke (1986) propose a multimodal treatment program, combining individual and group therapy. They approach the disturbed eating behavior through behavior therapeutic techniques and educational advice. In the group sessions, patients are given the chance to experiment with interpersonal relations. The therapy focuses on body perception and personal expression. Family problems related to the disturbed eating behavior are dealt with in family therapy sessions.

Andersen's (1985) eclectic approach is focused rather on making the symptomatic behavior superfluous than on its elimination. He distinguishes three areas:

1. Behavior therapy techniques are used to alter the abnormal eating behavior and other behavioral disturbances.
2. Medical treatment is required in case of low body weight and in complications of vomiting or purging.
3. Psychotherapy is focused on the psychological consequences of weight loss, low self-esteem, and underlying (psychodynamic) themes.

Abraham, Mason, and Mira (1985) propose an eclectic approach on account of the striking heterogeneity of BN. The therapy aims at changing attitudes about food and weight and at solving problems instead of the flight into bingeing. They use a cognitive-behavioral model, complemented with relaxation training and family therapy sessions (with emphasis on problems of independence or marital problems). Regarding other eclectic approaches, we refer to review articles by Garner and Fairburn (1987), Rosen (1987), and Oesterheld, McKenna, and Gould (1987), with the conclusion that a lot of these approaches need further evaluation.

Final Reflection

From the preceding discussion it should be clear that BN tends to cover a complex and multiform reality. In the evaluation of the different treatment models we always meet with two problems: the inadequate comparability of the concerned population of patients and the lack of methodologically reliable research (see also the qualitative review of 32 studies of individual and group treatment by

Cox & Meckel, 1989). It is far from being clear which of the described models will survive. Besides, the interest in the phenomenon is still too recent to let thorough research help us separate the wheat from the chaff. The accents in our own approach are based on personal preference and practical experience. In the following chapters, not just one model will be propagated as a panacea, but the value of ingredients from different therapy models will be recognized.

3

Treatment Planning

Clinical experience has taught us that a striking behavior such as bingeing is usually only the tip of the iceberg. Such an eating problem nearly always signals other problems. Hence, it seems to us that a treatment that is focused purely on the eating pathology offers few chances of succeeding. We try to make it clear to the patient that the bulimia is not "just there," but that the ever-recurring episodes of binge eating aim to signal something to the patient. We therefore invite patients to scrutinize their feelings preceding the bulimia to learn to discern its "hidden" significance and function in their personal life. The bulimia can signal problems on three different levels: individual, interactional, and sociocultural.

SIGNALING FUNCTION OF BULIMIA

The Individual Level

On the individual level, BN patients spontaneously mention that they often feel depressed and empty, sometimes even suicidal. Apart from mood fluctuations, self-mutilation, kleptomania (often the stealing of food, sometimes also of totally useless items), and alcohol abuse can occur. On the social level, their lives are often made up of chaos and ruin: rapidly changing and superficial contacts (sometimes including sexual promiscuity) or a total social isolation. In the latter case they spend their time at home with compulsive cleaning, cooking, and eating. The main problems for which they search for help are the irresistible binges and often also the accompanying feelings of depression. These complaints (binge eating and depression) can be used as a gateway to exploring the signaling function on the individual level.

> Myriam is 27 years of age and still lives with her parents. At the age of 18, she developed an obstinately concealed bulimia, which was first openly discussed in the family only a few months before her admission to our hospital. At the beginning of the therapy, her parents beg for help against their daughter's binges. Both patient and parents are told that the bulimia is not only a problem of excessive eating, but also a sign of something else being the matter. We stress the fact that the bulimia could appear to signal other problem areas, which the patient would like to change in her life. Via her diary (feelings preceding a binge) Myriam discovers, among others, the following problem areas:
>
> • Myriam's life in the family is very lonely and isolated. She has neither friends nor acquaintances. She has always avoided heterosexual contacts, though she has been feeling "a longing for a boyfriend" for several years.
> • After decreasing the number of binges, Myriam grows more conscious of her loneliness, but equally feels a growing, intense anger. This anger turns itself principally against her parents, who never encouraged her to make contacts outside the family. However, she does not dare to express her anger.
> • Myriam also finds out how little time she devotes to relaxation and leisure, in spite of the fact that she often feels restless. She has the feeling that relaxing or just quietly lazing away the day is evil or sinful.
>
> After several months of therapy, the bulimia not only acquires the status of an utterly destructive symptom against which she feels powerless, but Myriam also discovers why this bulimia has been haunting her life so long and persistently. The binges signal that

it's high time for her to take steps to break out of her solitude, to express her anger and make more time for herself and for leisure activities.

Elisa, a 24-year-old single woman who has had BN more than 12 years, is at her wits' end when she gets in touch with us. Because of her binge eating, she has become overweight (230 lb with a height of 68 inches), and for years she has been trying, with every (im)possible diet, to fight against her weight and binge eating. Via her diary and the individual therapy (in which hypnosis also is used, see Chapter 6), Elisa finds out that her eating problem is far more than just a diet problem or a struggle against the food addiction. She realizes that a sort of different person lives within her (she calls the person "Fatty"), who forces her to gorge herself and whom she has been fighting desperately for many years. When we get more closely acquainted with Fatty, it appears that the latter came into Elisa's life when she was faced with very painful, traumatizing experiences in her childhood: physical violence and forced sexual contact with a family member. Fatty used to invite Elisa to get some food in these moments, which made her feel more peaceful. This compulsive eating brought Elisa protection and security in these traumatizing situations. In the further development of the therapy, Elisa finds out how the continual distrust toward other people (especially men), the recurrent binges and mood swings, the suicidal thoughts, and the alcohol abuse are largely connected with those former traumatizing experiences. She now realizes that this must become the essential point of the treatment.

The Interactional Level

At first contact, patients will only rarely report a problem in their interactions, for instance, with their family or partner. Most patients describe the relations within the family as being excellent: They have very good parents or a wonderful spouse (friend) who is able to show unimaginable patience. BN patients often blame themselves for all the problems. In contract with this group, however, there is another group of BN patients who, even at the first interview, ascribe all of their problems to their unfortunate youth. Here the therapist feels the presence of enormous tension and conflict within the family from the first session. However, open or concealed, the significance of the bulimia on the interactional level should always be explored.

At the first family sessions, Myriam's family presents itself as an exemplary one. All of the family members seem to do their utmost to show their sympathy and concern for Myriam, to understand her, and to encourage her not to give up the treatment. But as soon as she acquires some control over her bingeing episodes, the tension within the family increases. Myriam is no longer the good and exemplary daughter. She begins to criticize the state of affairs in the family. She also tells how she has always felt herself overprotected in the family, how contacts with boys were always checked or labeled as evil. She becomes more aware of the strong feelings of loyalty toward her family. Conflicts are not allowed at home; anger and criticism are never to be expressed. The bulimia was a way to express somewhat this "forbidden" anger.

An important element is the parents' (principally the father's) strong pressure to perform exerted on Myriam. This has caused her an enormous fear of failure and, at the same time, a need to seek perfection in everything she does. In an individual session (which she requested herself), the mother dares to tell how lonely she feels in her relationship with her husband and how Myriam has always been her support and refuge. After a short time the facade of the ideal family collapses like a house of cards. The bulimia helped to maintain this dysfunctional family situation behind the mask of normality. The family members now discover that Myriam's bulimia implies a need for change for every one of them. The parents appear to be ready to change their attitude toward Myriam, but refuse to enter more deeply into the problems of their marital relationship.

At first, Elisa's family refuses every form of cooperation. They label her problems as "a lack of willpower." It is striking, however, that Elisa binges mainly when she goes to her family during the weekends. Via the diary, Elisa finds out how she is again and again overcome with feelings of powerlessness, guilt, and anxiety in those moments, which remind her of the traumatizing past, whereafter she starts bingeing. She therefore decides to stay away from her family, at least for the time being. This appears to be the only way to detach herself emotionally and to protect her from the family context. It should also enable her to cope with her traumas via individual therapy.

The Sociocultural Level

Though for various reasons few reliable data are as yet available on the exact prevalence of bulimia in the Western world, one may certainly assume that the occurrence of eating disorders has increased in the last two decades. In our opinion, this increase should be connected with the changed social position of women. Our social system subjects women to a pattern of high pressure and expectations. On the one hand, a female is still supposed to become a mother and the boss in the kitchen, and to manage the major part of the children's education and the responsibility for the household. On the other hand, women demand not only economic independence, but also professional achievement. However, in "a man's world" success often means being pretty, slender, and sexy. The obsessional preoccupation with food and body weight may signal this field of tension between contradictory expectations and demands that modern women have to meet nowadays. It strikes us regularly how anorexia and bulimia patients engage in a battle with their family, precisely in the woman's traditional realm: the kitchen. Many patients cook fancy things for hours on end and sometimes force the other family members to consume their culinary masterpieces!

In the therapy, it will therefore be important to teach patients to look critically at the various expectations on the social level. The bulimia is then seen as a signal of one's self-dissatisfaction, lacking individuality, and complying too much with idealized images of others. For some, this will mean that they will have to put certain study or work plans to a thorough discussion. For others, it implies detaching themselves from a self-image programmed by their family or partner. In our experience group therapy is preeminently appropriate to stimulate this sort of self-criticism regarding social role and future expectations (see Chapter 5).

FUNCTIONAL ANALYSIS

The first chapter was devoted to the diagnostic characteristics of BN, as described in DSM-III-R. A functional analysis of the bulimic issue obviously comprises more than just finding out whether the described characteristics are present or not in a particular patient. In a thorough functional analysis, the therapist should collect information on the different levels of the patient's functioning. The therapist should not only analyze the patient's eating (bingeing) behavior and psychological functioning, but also assess the family and/or marital system.

Gathering Information

The most obvious method is the *clinical interview*. At the very first contact the patient's parents and/or partner are preferably present. This is intended to make it clear to the family and the partner from the very beginning that we need their cooperation in the treatment. During this initial contact, the patient is first interviewed together with the family or the partner, and subsequently the various subsystems (patient, parents, siblings) are seen separately. It is recommendable to collect and arrange the information in a standardized way. For this purpose, we have developed a scale: the Eating Disorder Evaluation Scale (EDES; Vandereycken 1987c), which gives a global clinical score on the seriousness of the issue; the lower the score, the more pathological the level of dysfunctioning of patients (see Appendix A).

Apart from the interview we also make use of standardized questionnaires:

- The *Eating Disorders Inventory* (EDI; Garner, Olmsted, & Polivy, 1983) measures various typical characteristics of eating disorder patients, such as the urge to be thin, perfectionism, and body dissatisfaction.
- The *Body Attitudes Questionnaire* (BAQ; Van Coppenolle, Probst, Vandereycken, Goris, & Meermann, 1990) measures specific aspects of body experience, such as attention to body size, familiarity with one's own body, and comparison of body appearance.
- The *Symptom Check-List* (SCL-90; Derogatis, 1977) measures specific complementary complaints, such as depression, anxiety, hostility, and somatization.
- The *Leuven Family Questionnaire* (Vandereycken et al., 1989) measures three different family characteristics: cohesion, conflict, and adaptability.

In the evaluation of these questionnaires one should always consider the fact that eating disorder patients often do not fill in such questionnaires very accurately or reliably; this goes especially for anorexia nervosa patients (Vandereycken & Vanderlinden, 1983). The data should therefore be interpreted with the necessary caution and reserve.

Apart from the interview and the questionnaires, all patients are asked to keep a *diary* (see Chapter 4). In this diary is noted a detailed description of the eating behavior, bulimia, vomiting, and/or purging and also the accompanying thoughts, feelings, and activities. The diary is a basic element in the assessment of the patient's problems and has to be filled out during the whole treatment. Since we feel the need to clearly define treatment objectives during the first assessment phase, we have developed the *Goal Attainment Evaluation* (see Appendix B). This is a specifically therapy-oriented assessment procedure, used in both inpatient and outpatient treatment. The patients are asked to describe problem areas on three different levels (symptoms, self-experience, interactions) and also to determine three different small but concrete steps for each problem area that may help to solve this specific problem (for application, see Chapter 5). Problem areas, objectives, and concrete steps will mostly change as a function of the treatment phase that patients are in. In the initial phase, special attention will be paid to the typical eating problems. In a further phase, the problem areas on the level of self-perception and interactions will be the focus (Vandereycken, Vanderlinden, & Van Werde, 1986; Vanderlinden & Vandereycken, 1988b). We wish to recommend strongly this assessment procedure, since it has certain unmistakable advantages:

- In the first place, patients are invited to draft their own treatment objectives. The assessment is focused very strongly on the patients' own responsibility.
- The Goal Attainment Evaluation immediately makes a link between assessment and treatment. Patients are asked to draft a treatment plan, emphasizing again their responsibility.

A last procedure, meant to collect information on the family's functioning or the place occupied by the patient in the family, is the *family portrait*. Patients are asked to make a drawing (or collage) of their family: how they perceive their position in the family and how they see mutual relationships. The expression of this may also be symbolic (e.g., animals or a group of trees; see Vandereycken et al., 1989).

Functional Analysis of the Individual

The first step in the functional analysis is the assessment of the bulimia. When BN patients ask for help, it is often after the binges, vomiting, and/or purging have taken complete control of their life.

> When Ann wakes up around 6 in the morning, she almost automatically goes into the kitchen. Here, she gorges herself as quick as lightning with bread and sweets. After that, she feels very tense, goes to the toilet, and experiences a sort of relief and release when all the food is thrown up quite easily. In the last weeks, this bingeing-vomiting cycle has been repeated some 10 times a day. When she suddenly started vomiting blood, she panicked and asked for help for the first time.

With regard to the *binges* the following questions can be asked:

- Is the urge to binge (un)controllable?
- What is the frequency of the binges?
- In what situations do they occur?
- What sort of food is consumed?
- What does the patient do just before and after the binge?
- Does the patient vomit after bingeing?
- Is the vomiting self-induced or does it happen automatically?
- How often does the patient vomit, and how long is it put off after bingeing?
- Does the patient take laxatives, diuretics, or appetite suppressants? If so, which products, how often, and in what dose?
- Does the patient exercise regularly, and is the patient hyperactive after the meal?

In connection with the *general eating pattern*:

- How many meals does the patient consume daily?
- At what times are the meals eaten?
- What kinds of food does the patient eat during normal meals?

- Which foods (candy) are avoided?
- Does the patient collect or hoard any food?
- Does the patient vomit or purge even after a normal meal?
- Does the patient also eat or nibble between meals?
- Does the patient fast or diet during the day?

In connection with the patient's *weight*:

- What is the patient's present weight?
- Does the patient have weight fluctuations?
- Does the patient have a past history of obesity or anorexia nervosa? If so, at what age?
- What have been the patient's highest and lowest weights?
- How frequently has the patient gone on a diet?
- What is the patient's desired weight ("ideal" weight)?
- How does the patient perceive the present weight and body shape?

Apart from the bulimia, vomiting, and/or purging and the strong preoccupation with body shape, weight, and eating pattern, BN patients may show a series of *other important problem areas*, which they often do not mention spontaneously in the first sessions:

- Is the patient depressed? Has the patient suicidal thoughts or plans? Does the patient feel "empty" at times?
- Has the patient mood swings?
- Does the patient abuse alcohol, drugs, or pills?
- Is there an urge for self-mutilation?
- Is the patient very anxious or tense?
- Does the patient steal food, money, or other things?
- Has the patient any "blackouts" after a binge? Does the patient sometimes fail to remember what happened before the binge?
- Is the patient sometimes disordered? Does the patient expe-

rience hallucinations, hear voices, or sometimes have disturbed memory or perception?
* Has the patient any sexual problems?

Jean becomes very anxious and depressed in the evening and in those moments mostly wishes she was dead. She starts drinking alcohol and goes roaming about in the streets as soon as it gets dark. She is in search of food (often tainted food she hoards or swallows at home). "Almost like a starved animal," Jean tells us. In the morning she regularly wakes up in a blackout: She completely fails to remember what she did the evening and night before.

Also the *psychosocial and personal functioning* should be thoroughly evaluated:

* In what circumstances does the patient live?
* Does the patient have a job or study? What is the patient's educational level?
* How does the patient spend leisure time?
* Has the patient any hobbies or other activities?
* Has the patient good social contacts?
* How does the patient function compared to peers?
* How is the patient's relationship with the family of origin (parents, siblings)?
* How does the patient describe himself or herself? Are there any irrational beliefs and exaggerated self-criticism?
* Does the patient act very impulsively?
* Is the patient inclined to black-and-white, all-or-none reasoning?
* Has the patient ever been emotionally shocked or traumatized (e.g., physical abuse, rape, or incest)?

In the intake interview, the *patient's readiness to change* should be thoroughly evaluated (see Chapter 4). An apparently enthusiastic reaction in the beginning of treatment may be very misleading.

Patients should be asked to give treatment priority in their daily life, and the therapist should put their motivation and engagement to the test as soon as possible. Though patients often expect quick relief, many of them are afraid to detach themselves completely from the bulimia, and the direct consequences of a real change in their lives fill them with fear. The following questions are important in this respect:

- Has the bulimia any positive results for you? Does the bulimia help you to stay away from certain things you are afraid of?
- Can you imagine a life without bulimia? Would a life without bulimia have any disadvantages for you? How quickly and drastically do you want to stop bingeing, vomiting, or purging?

Obviously, a *thorough medical history and physical examination* should always be planned. The bingeing, vomiting, and purging can be a serious threat to the physical functioning of the patient (see Table 2, Chapter 1). The patient should be well informed about this—for example, by means of an information brochure (see Appendix C)—since many patients appear to ignore or deny all harmful consequences and dangers.

Functional Analysis of the Family or Marital System

The family and/or partner are to be invited to preferably the first interview, in order to give them the message that their cooperation in the treatment is very important. In the assessment of the family system special attention is paid to:

- the place of the symptom within the family (or marriage);
- the specific characteristics of family/marital interactions; and
- the psychosocial functioning and possible (psycho)pathology in all family members.

The following questions are aimed at gaining insight into the *family's/partner's perception* of the origin, development, and possible solution of the problem:

- Which family members know about the bulimia and since when?
- What are the views of the individual family members (partner) on the bulimia or other problems they want solved?
- Can the family members (partner) also suggest certain causes for the development of the bulimia?
- How have family members (partner) already tried to solve the problem?
- Has help already been asked for from outside?
- Which family member is most concerned about the bulimia?
- Does the family (partner) already have an idea or suggestion about a possible way to solve the eating problem?

In Tania's family, the cause of the bulimia is placed completely outside of the family. The parents are convinced that there is no other problem whatsoever at home. They say that their daughter's inability to deal with exam stress made her binge and vomit secretly. They have never tried to solve the problem themselves but always resorted to medical help: Tania has already been briefly treated some 10 times by an internist. Her brother keeps entirely in the background in the presence of the parents.

Family Structure

Often bulimia is found in either utterly closed families with a strong demarcation from the outside world, or families that are rather chaotic, with no boundaries at all. The therapist tries to gain insight into the mutual coalitions:

- Who reacts when the patient starts bingeing?
- Do they talk openly about the bingeing and vomiting?

- Are the bingeing and vomiting a family secret or are there nonrelatives who know about it?
- Whom does the patient ask for support?

Life Cycle of the Family

The families of bulimics are usually in a significant transitional phase: Children have become adolescents or young adults and are either about to leave or have already left the house. The leaving home of the children often creates a great emptiness for the mother, which can render the marital relationship more important again. The parents have to reorganize and intensify their marital relationship.

These changes bring about a lot of tensions and conflicts. The therapist should inquire about the following:

- In which phase of the life cycle is the family?
- Are there any children who live apart from the family? How did this go off?
- How did the parents separate themselves from their family of origin? How did they feel when they left their family?
- Has the patient already tried to live independently?

Conflict Solution Capacity

Many families seldom or never succeed in finding a solution for the internal tensions and conflicts. These are either hushed up or openly "fought out" with escalating quarrels and sometimes physical violence. The therapist should find out:

- Is someone angry with the child because of the bulimia?
- Is this anger expressed and how?
- How does the family deal with anger, tensions, and conflicts?
- Can this anger lead to physical violence?

- Who is most frightened when the father and/or the mother gets angry?

Intergenerational Aspects

We often ascertain that the grandparents still exert a strong influence on the family of the BN patient (e.g., they live in the immediate neighborhood or even in the family home). It appears that in many cases parents were traumatized in their childhood, for example, by the early loss of a significant family member. Not seldom the parents themselves seem to have been affectively neglected in their family of origin. The therapist should therefore check whether intergenerational influences still bear on the family system and to what extent:

- What did the parents learn about marriage, education, and so on in their family of origin?
- How is the relationship of the parents with their families of origin?
- Did the parents experience emotional traumas in their family of origin?
- What did the parents and grandparents expect from the patient as a child or as a future adult? Do these expectations resemble (unfulfilled) hopes or (frustrated) expectations they cherished for themselves?

Function of the Bulimia Within the Family System

One of the central questions is whether and to what extent the bulimia has a function or significance in the family or marital system (see also Chapter 7). Does the bulimia act as a lightning rod for concealed tensions and conflicts in the marital (parental) relationship? Is the bulimia a signal of serious boundary exceeding in the family or of too rigid demarcation with regard to the outside world? Is the bulimia the only way to express aggression within this family? Do the bingeing and vomiting mean that the patient feels quite ill at ease with the partner? If the patient stopped bingeing, what could it change in family relations, or in the patient's relationship with the partner? Would it have more (positive or negative) consequences for certain family members than for others?

The therapist should also consider the detection of *psychopathology in other family members*. The following problems are often found in grandparents, parents, and siblings: eating disorders, depression, alcoholism, obsessive-compulsive disorder, psychotic episodes, and aggressive outbursts. The presence of serious pathology in the other family members will also be an important consideration in the decision whether the patient should be hospitalized or not.

INPATIENT VS. OUTPATIENT TREATMENT

Until today, little attention had been paid in the literature to the question when outpatient therapy is at its limits and inpatient treatment becomes unavoidable. In the treatment reviews (e.g., Garner & Fairburn, 1987; Fairburn, 1988), inpatient and outpatient treatment are discussed without any clear indications. Fairburn (1985) and Abraham and colleagues (1985) consider high risk of suicide and life-threatening health as indications for hospitalization. We would like to add two important indications: first, those patients who live in a highly conflictual family situation, reinforcing a vicious circle between the bulimia and the interactional conflicts and, second, those patients who suffer from serious social isolation and for whom, because of lack of social control, the bulimic behavior has become an automatized ritual to fill up the "empty" time. Inpatient treatment, on the other hand, may have serious disadvantages and limitations (see Chapter 8). Nevertheless, it seems indicated in the following cases:

1. The patient's physical condition is alarming (see Chapter 1).
2. There is a serious risk of suicide.
3. The patient has *"multisymptomatic"* BN, in which there is not only a disturbed eating pattern, but also problems in impulse control like drug abuse (amphetamines), alcohol abuse, self-mutilation, kleptomania, obsessive-compulsive disorder, and sexual disinhibition. Frequently we find a personality disorder of the borderline type linked to this psychopathologic behavior. In this group of patients the manipulation of food is associated to a varying degree with alcohol and drug abuse. These patients use them interchangeably and in similar ways. The "choice" they make depends on their attitude toward drugs, alcohol, and food. Amphetamines are used as a suppressor of the urge to binge. A series of different drugs may be used as a way to control the fear of becoming fat (laxatives, diuretics, so-called natural products) or as a remedy for the consequences of the disturbed eating patterns (e.g., sleeping pills). Alcohol use may have different motives or functions: (a) to block the urge to eat, (b) to replace food bingeing, (c) to suppress the dysphoric mood before or after binge eating, or (d) to induce a loss of control (alcohol as excuse). The stealing of food is sometimes explained by the financial problems caused by extreme or expensive bulimic behavior or is embedded in a ritual that precedes the bulimic behavior. Patients may also show obsessive-compulsive behavior patterns in daily life (job, household). The disturbed eating acts then as a relief from these rituals. Some patients also have periods of sexual disinhibition. A fear of going out of control leads them to seek "safe" relationships. The choice of the partner is less important than the underlying meaning: The partner is used as protection or safety against the emptiness in their life. This is a way of seeking sexual release without meaningful com-

mitment. In this way, they consume sex (or men) as they do food, alcohol, or drugs.

4. The patient's parents are difficult to motivate to engage in treatment, which may occur for the following reasons:

   • Denial of the severity of the physical and psychological consequences of bulimia
   • Parental psychopathology in the past or present (depression, addiction)
   • Persistent (overt or subtle) triangulation within the family, manipulating the patient in parental conflicts (e.g., divorce battles)

   These can lead to a disturbed family context, where there exists a vicious circle between the bulimic behavior and the interactional conflicts.

5. The patient lives in extreme social isolation as a result of the time- and energy-consuming bulimia. It can reach such an importance that the whole day is planned around binge eating. All leisure time is consecrated to food; social activities and contacts are diminished or even completely avoided. If the patient lives alone, there is no social control by family members or friends, which makes it even more difficult to restrict the bulimic urge. Life becomes more chaotic, and with the conviction no one will understand them, patients isolate themselves more and more. As such, however, they create even more time alone, that is, a new occasion for bulimia: The vicious circle is closed.

In one or more of these situations outpatient treatment is risky or very likely to fail. Admission to a hospital (preferably a specialized center) can be seen then as a temporary but necessary disruption of a malignant behavioral pattern. It is a sort of detoxification that permits building a more solid basis for further outpatient therapy. Sometimes the decision to hospitalize is postponed far too long because of the resistances of both the patient and the family. They are often unaware of the seriousness and complexity of the issue. In these cases we prefer to start an outpatient therapy anyway, but with a time-limited (2 or 3 months) written contract in which the necessary preparedness is formulated in terms of minimal change in behavior. In cases where the patient lives together with a partner or family, we make these contracts in their presence. The expected behavior changes are formulated in terms of resuming a healthy eating pattern and a control over the bulimic ritual ("controlled eating" instead of complete abstinence).

We always give the patient the benefit of the doubt. We continue outpatient treatment, if the patient can convince us of its usefulness in the next 2 or 3 months by reaching the proposed goals; if not, we stop the therapy and inpatient treatment becomes unavoidable. For some patients this acts as an extra stimulus to attempt a breakthrough in their chaotic eating pattern. Others become aware that they are more deeply stuck in their problems than they thought, and realize that the continuation of an outpatient treatment can lead only to more disappointments.

Therefore the outpatient therapy can have a *motivational function:* The patient may gain some insight into the meanings and functions of the bulimic behavior. In this way the patient might be able to consider inpatient treatment not as a sign of failure but as a "new chance." It will act as a turning point, breaking through an unescapable vicious circle. Afterward many patients tell us that they experienced the admission as a sort of stay in a foster family and that they could probably never have broken through the spiral of bingeing and vomiting without it.

PHARMACOTHERAPY

We will briefly discuss our opinion regarding the use of psychotropic drugs in BN. The role of medication in eating disorders is still a controversial subject (see Garfinkel & Garner, 1987; Goldbloom, Kennedy, Kaplan, & Woodside, 1989). The use of antidepressants in particular has become a central element in the discussion about a possible relationship between BN and mood disorders (see Chapter 2). In recent years many antidepressants have been tested in bulimic patients, but few studies have been well controlled and results are equivocal. The interpretation of the research data appears to depend largely on the attitude of the clinicians involved: Some are very enthusiastic (e.g., Hudson & Pope, 1990), while others remain skeptical (e.g., Mitchell, 1988). Antidepressants, and especially serotonin reuptake blockers (e.g., fluoxetine), may have beneficial effects on both mood and eating behavior, but only in a subgroup of bulimics and only in the short run. Indeed, the characteristics of the "responders" are not known yet, and no long-term follow-up studies are available yet (many patients appear to relapse after withdrawal of the medication). Moreover, the use of antidepressants is not without problems or risks. Many bulimics have difficulty in treatment compliance: They may either forget to take their pills or undo the possible effect by their purging behavior. Other patients may already have a tendency toward drug abuse, while still others might be suicidal, with the danger of taking an overdose. Finally, one should be cautious from a psychotherapeutic viewpoint: These patients tend to reason in all-or-none terms, with the tendency to ascribe personal changes to external events. This attitude may be reinforced by the taking of a drug: Their responsibility for changing their life-style is avoided then since "the drug will do all the work."

Taking this cost/benefit issue into consideration from a purely practical viewpoint and relying on our own clinical experience, we recommend pharmacotherapy only in the following cases and under the condition that it should be combined with some form of appropriate psychotherapy:

- In BN patients who show a concomitant mood disorder without clear connection with the disturbed eating behavior, as demonstrated by a psychotherapeutically induced improvement of the eating pattern without concomitant amelioration in mood
- In BN patients whose clear symptoms of depression are most probably related to their eating behavior and psychosocial situation, but who because of this seriously disordered mood find it very difficult to (be motivated to) engage in psychotherapy
- In BN patients where forms of psychotherapy, regardless of their skillful application and the honest engagement of the patient, have failed

4

Individual Therapy

We shall successively sketch the formal characteristics of an out-patient individual therapy, the motivation for treatment, and the course of the therapy, with special attention to the therapeutic pitfalls.

GENERAL CHARACTERISTICS

In most cases the seriousness of the disorder necessitates that sessions take place twice a week during a period of 2 or 3 months. The objective in the first phase is twofold. First, a well-balanced eating pattern (three meals and two snacks) is built up, and the bulimic eating pattern is brought under control according to a nonabstinence approach. This means that a progressive reduction of the bingeing-vomiting cycles should be achieved. Second, this period offers the therapist a lot of information on the life situation of the patient, which will help in working out a functional analysis of the bulimic behavior. An interview with the partner and/or the family (even when the patient lives apart from them) also takes place, so that the therapist can inquire about the patient's relationship with the partner or the family of origin. If they are not informed about the bulimia, this situation constitutes a primary motivational task for the patient, who must now bring the problem into the open at home. Frequently, it is the first time that the secret bulimic behavior is revealed in all candor. The therapist makes the partner/family aware of the seriousness of BN and the necessity of treatment (if necessary, with concrete agreements). This smoothes the path to involve the partner/family in the treatment in the next phase, if necessary. It is not always easy in an outpatient setting to get their collaboration. Many adopt a defensive attitude and feel very uneasy at the idea of being involved in the discussion and alteration of this bizarre eating behavior. But it is our experience that this cooperation is very important in order to avoid having patients drop out at the inevitable crises during treatment.

The individual therapy is of limited duration. If it evolves favorably, we then prefer to switch patients over to group therapy (with

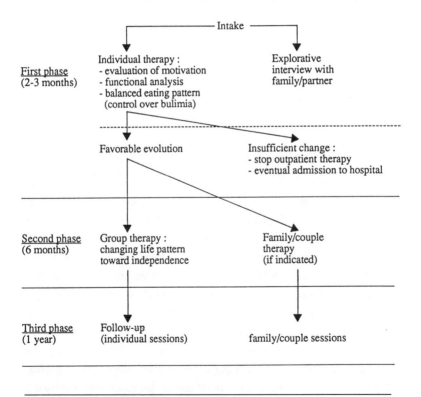

Figure 2. Course of Outpatient Therapy.

parallel family or couple therapy). If the first phase is unfavorable, outpatient therapy is stopped according to the therapeutic contract and can be followed by an admission to a specialized eating disorders unit (see Chapter 8). The purpose of group therapy (phase 2) is to achieve effective changes in the patient's life toward independence so that the bulimia becomes superfluous (see Chapter 5). The family/couple therapy attempts to facilitate the therapeutic process (see Chapter 7). This second phase takes on average 6 months (sometimes up to 1 year). Finally, we plan a follow-up (phase 3) aimed at the consolidation of the achieved changes. This again takes place on an individual basis, and the sessions are progressively spread out in time. The partner or the family can be involved in this follow-up as well. The duration varies but takes at least 1 year (see Chapter 9).

We ascertain that patients do not always go easily through the phase transitions in the treatment program; a temporary relapse of the bulimic behavior is often observed, usually at crucial moments of the therapy.

ASSESSING MOTIVATION FOR CHANGE

At the beginning special attention must be paid to the motivation of these patients. They often suffer badly from the ever-recurring binges and want to get rid of them as soon as possible. This apparent willingness for a quick and drastic change is a first pitfall for the therapist. A lot of patients expect direct and almost magic therapeutic interventions. This clearly reflects their unrealistic expectations and achievement orientation. We try to convince them that the bulimic episode is not an enemy, but an ally; it is a signal that something is going "wrong" in their life (see Chapter 3). Unfortunately, most patients don't realize the severity and complexity of their problems. They reduce the problem to a wrong eating habit. Reinforcing this idea by jumping too quickly into the presented problem with therapeutic techniques leads to their prematurely dropping out.

The patients must be confronted with the severity of their problems. First, we give them information on the psychological and physical consequences of the bulimic behavior. We let them read a brochure or book about eating disorders (see Appendix C). We state that treatment has a chance of succeeding only when it becomes top priority in their lives. This is embedded in the structure of our approach. The first months of treatment we ask them to come twice a week, with the explicit rule that there is no good excuse to be absent from the sessions; otherwise their engagement will be questioned. Second, patients have to keep a diary of their eating pattern and associated activities, feelings, and thoughts. Third, we make clear that the goal of treatment is not the quick disappearance of the bulimic behavior. Success in the long run is better guaranteed when there is a gradual decrease of the bulimia, with a growing understanding of the meanings of this behavior. Most patients are afraid to detach themselves completely from the bulimia; the direct consequences of a real change in their lives evoke fears. Hence, fourth, their readiness for change should be tested: positive and negative consequences of a life without bulimia (see Chapter 3).

Doris (18 years old) seeks help for her bulimia (lasting for 5 years) because she feels ashamed and disgusted about her body (35 lb overweight). She is overenthusiastic because she heard about the good results of our approach from a school friend. When we ask how her life would look without bulimia, she cannot give an answer. Then she gets the usual homework task to write down the advantages and disadvantages of stopping the bingeing. Here's her list:

Advantages

• More self-respect, no disgust about myself anymore

- To have time for things I want to do (take care of myself, buy clothes, exercise, and dance)
- No desire anymore to escape from myself
- To cope normally with food
- No more social isolation
- To have normal relationships without fear or shame
- To like my own body and to enjoy sex again

Disadvantages

- It no longer releases my aggression (toward others and myself).
- I lose my strategy against loneliness.
- I cannot shock other people (especially mother) anymore.
- Who will I be without my problem?
- I'm afraid to become proud of myself.
- I'll feel empty and depressed.

When discussing this list, she admits to being astonished about what she has discovered about her bulimia. She realizes that her problems are far more complex than she thought and that it will be difficult to find other coping strategies for her negative feelings.

Finally, we point out that this outpatient therapy might fail as well. If an obvious improvement in the eating pattern does not occur within 2 months, this would mean that this approach has been unsuccessful. This would imply that outpatient therapy should be stopped and that a hospitalization should be considered.

The *nonabstinence approach* is an essential point of our outpatient treatment (see Bemis, 1985). In view of the specific cognitive and emotional styles of these patients, a quick attack on and victory over the bulimic behavior only consolidates their absolutistic standards, their unrealistic planning, and their dichotomous all-or-none thinking. The first bulimic relapse (which is often unavoidable) is seen as another failure and reinforces their feelings of insufficiency and inferiority. And even if patients succeed in suddenly stopping bingeing and vomiting at the beginning of the treatment, they create for themselves an "as if" reality in which all their problems are seemingly resolved. We remain skeptical about this success and predict that the bulimic behavior will come back. Besides, such a bulimic relapse can be an important signal of concealed problems (see Chapter 3). Because of their perfectionist attitude and their incapacity to accept their own weak or negative aspects, patients again and again try to induce the therapist to take care of the binges as soon as possible.

- "I want to get rid of those binges as soon as possible, because I think it's horrible."
- "If you help me to get rid of those binges, I will stop vomiting automatically and I will eat normally like everybody else."
- "I can only feel happy if I have no binges."
- "I am only satisfied with the past day if I have had no binges."

If therapists comply with this sometimes compelling request, they will create more experiences of failure with undesirable consequences for the already fragile self-esteem of patients and will risk their dropping out prematurely. When therapists repeatedly confront patients with the risk of another (the umpteenth) failure in their life, the patients will slowly accept the step-by-step approach. But some patients will attempt to progress faster. The disappointments that probably result lead to an increase of the bulimic behavior, with a greater likelihood of dropout.

Marilyn, a 28-year-old unmarried woman, is working as a representative in a computer firm. During the time she lived at home, she usually was on some diet. Five years ago, when she left home to live on her own, the bingeing and vomiting started. Every evening this bulimic behavior was a time-consuming ritual. She slept so little that her work began to suffer. She had problems with her memory and concentration; she made unusual mistakes, so that her colleagues asked annoying questions. Very ashamed of this behavior, she did the best she could to hide it from those around her (including her family). Because it became even more hard for her to conceal that there was something wrong, she looked for professional help. She demanded that there be a dramatic change in her eating pattern in order to convince those around her of her apparent health. Always she strived for higher goals than the ones agreed upon during the session. In this way she created for herself new failures: Instead of decreasing, the bulimic ritual augmented as a solace for the disappointments. She became anxious that therapy wouldn't work, but could not realize the undermining impact of her attitude on possible therapeutic changes. She avoided the confrontation of being, once again, a "loser" by staying away from therapy without any communication.

CHANGING THE EATING PATTERN

The first step in changing the eating behavior is not directly focused on decreasing the bingeing-vomiting cycles, but rather on teaching a sound and well-balanced eating pattern, which is necessary to bring the bulimia under control. Otherwise, the therapy would "help" patients to achieve the favorite anorexic state!

Marian, a 27-year-old secretary who lives on her own, has had problems with food for 7 years. After 6 years' history of anorexia nervosa, she started to binge and vomit. Yet she still attempts to return to her anorexia period, for then she felt a lot better and now she considers herself a failure because of the bingeing. She tries to be anorexic by hardly giving herself the time to eat something in the morning. She takes some low-fat yogurt, one single sandwich without filling, and an apple to her work but tries to postpone lunch as long as possible. She does so by working with extreme zeal; she even begrudges herself a coffee break. When she gets to her apartment in the evening, she starts cleaning and tidying it up. As soon as that is done, she throws herself on the food till it is time to go to bed.

Since BN patients experience a real and marked loss of control over food, frequent use is made of self-control techniques (which can be completed by hypnotic techniques; see Chapter 6) in order to stimulate and consolidate the necessary changes. One shows self-control if one demonstrates a behavior of which the expected chance to choose that particular behavior is smaller than the likelihood of preferring alternative available behaviors. Because the treatment is focused on giving the patients as much responsibility as possible for making changes, the application of self-control techniques offers some advantages:

- The problem-solving capacity is enlarged. In this way, patients learn to discover functional connections between their bulimic behavior and their life situation.
- The chances of maintenance and generalization of the achieved improvement are enlarged. This is important because the change process is accompanied by regular ups and downs.
- The emphasis lies on carrying out in one's daily life the agreements made in the therapy sessions. It is necessary that patients try to bring about concrete and effective changes in their eating pattern so that their feeling of control over their eating behavior increases.

The guideline in the enhancement of the control over the eating behavior is the diary. The patient is asked to keep a detailed diary according to a standardized scheme: description of the daily eating pattern (all consumed foods and drinks described in daily form of consumption, without counting calories or weighing food), connected activities, accompanying thoughts and feelings. This forms for the patients a first but essential confrontation with their disturbed eating behavior. Moreover, this is a way to break through the clandestinity around bingeing and purging. They are often ashamed to write down everything they have consumed in a binge. Some are afraid to be punished (as a matter of fact, they continually do this themselves through self-reproaches), while others see themselves confronted with the hopelessness of their situation. An honest report is a conditio sine qua non. We warn them that they might feel the tendency to deform the information about the bulimic behavior. We accentuate therefore that it is, in the first place, a matter of collecting as much information as possible, so as to enable us to draft an efficient and purposeful treatment plan. Moreover, it is pointed out to them that the extent of their bulimic behavior is no criterion whatsoever of the severity of their problems and does not determine the prognosis. Honesty with oneself (in the diary) is absolutely required, to give the therapy a chance of succeeding. In this respect, they are often told not to try to change their eating practices during this self-monitoring phase, as these will not last and may discourage the efforts they will be expected to make in the therapy. The diary offers much information, both on the eating behavior and the context wherein binges occur and on accompanying ideas, conceptions, and feelings of patients.

Christine, a 29-year-old woman, started a radical diet 12 years ago. This became uncontrollable and she went into an anorexic period. Two years later she switched into periods of fasting alternated by binges that made her weight shoot way up. A year ago she discovered by coincidence the way to vomit and began to abuse laxatives. The binges increased and her weight began to decrease. This hampered her social life and her work gave her no satisfaction anymore. A friend she met a few months before the therapy is the only one who knows about her problem. We produce a fragment of her diary at the beginning of the therapy (see the following pages).

In this phase of treatment, patients are thoroughly informed about BN and about its harmful effects both physically and psychologically (see Appendix C). For some, this can be sufficient to abruptly cease vomiting or purging (but not bingeing). The bingeing-vomiting cycle is what catches the eye the most in the eating pat-

Christine's Diary (V = vomiting, L = laxatives)

Time	Consumed Food, Drinks	Place	V/L	Context (activities, feelings, and thoughts)	
				Before	After
6:30 A.M.	2 cups of black coffee	Kitchen		Since I ate much more than I would allow myself to do last night, I only wanted to have black coffee this morning. I didn't ask myself if I was hungry or not.	
8:00 A.M.		Living room		The scale showed 136 lb. I thought this was too much, so I had to go down.	
11:40 A.M.	1 butter biscuit, 1 handful of puffs, 1 lasagne, 1 can of fried potatoes, 1 can of peas and carrots, 1 fried egg, 7	Living room		This binge had been haunting my mind for quite a long time. Because of my work and the relation with my friend, I have very little space for a good binge.	Now I feel very guilty: because of the waste of money, but also because I have again wasted so many hours of my life, and escaped from reality, being no part of the

Continued . . .

Today, I had to hear exams and the very moment I got out of bed and even since yesterday I have been calculating: I shall need about that much to hear those exams. It'll take 2 hours to binge and vomit and to come back to my senses again. Tonight at 6 all must be done, for I'll have to meet my friend at the station. I was anxious to get over with the exams (I couldn't care less what they answered), then I drove quickly to the store and while I was driving home, I was totally absorbed by the idea of stuffing myself. I'd have let nobody bother me, the whole world could go to hell, I feel and want just one thing: eating. What is

sandwiches with 1½ slices of cheese and 3 or 4 slices of ham, 2 or 3 spoonfuls of mayonnaise, 8 sandwiches with a lot of chocolate spread, 2 butter biscuits and a creamed corn, 7 or 8 chocolate cookies, a lot of butter on each sandwich, 6 bottles of beer

outside world, because it happened once again. Afterward, I weighed myself. The scales showed something between 134 and 135 lb. This was more or less comforting: Everything's gone out again. I feel uncomfortable now. After bingeing and vomiting I won't eat for the rest of the day, but tonight I'll have to eat with William and I already begin to panic now.

8:30 P.M.	1 sandwich with just a little bit of low-fat margarine and a half slice of cheese and mustard, 1 tomato, a few slices of cucumber, black coffee	Living room	so frustrating and rotten about vomiting is that I don't even remember how much I have eaten already and how much I will be able to eat. My eating scheme, as it has been worked out in my mind, gets even more confused. I was hungry again, but I binged 13 hours ago and I am very fond of sandwiches, bread rolls, or slices of bread with cheese. I ate with William, but as a matter of fact, I didn't enjoy the food for different reasons. Because I thought to myself: Would it be too much or not? Because I want to make it as long as possible, for when I've	My hunger is somewhat checked, but, in a way, I don't feel really satisfied, and I'm also really panicking because I'll absolutely have to try not to eat too much before I turn in, because tomorrow I'll be able to catch up much less easily.

Continued . . . .

had this sandwich, it'll be over till straight before bedtime. I want to eat less than my table companions. Eating during the day is difficult, because I want to save it for the evening. Whenever I've had a binge, I have to make a great effort to remember what I have eaten: It all happens so quickly and without thinking, totally secluded from myself and the world, that I can hardly remember what I have eaten afterward.

9:00 P.M.

I'm already considering what I'll be *allowed* to eat right away.

11:00 P.M.

I have the feeling I can never do it right, that I'm always disappointing other people, that they

			have different expectations, and that I don't come up to them. I feel so toward William and my family and yet I'm already constantly forgetting what I really want myself.	
0:00	A saucer of low-fat soft cheese and 1 currant bun	Bedroom	I could allow myself to eat this, and my stomach was fairly grumbling.	I had to fight very hard to stop eating. But I wanted to have more, much more, and I couldn't go to sleep immediately, and I started thinking about all the food that is still in the cupboard and that I could eat with an excuse: Tomorrow I'll skip breakfast and lunch. I didn't do it, because I would probably get the feeling of having lost another battle.

tern of BN patients, but we know that these patients, in spite of their loss of control, go through intermittent periods of restrictive eating (dieting). If patients wish to succeed in controlling their binges, it is essential that they should abandon these periods of fasting by acquiring a normal eating pattern (three varied meals and two snacks). This appears to be very threatening to most patients because of their fear of becoming fat. Yet they should realize that the starving is also responsible for provoking and maintaining the binges. The fact that these changes are accompanied by a slight increase in weight, which almost automatically disappears afterward, is explained to them beforehand, with reference to the principles of body metabolism and inevitable accompanying weight variations (see Chapter 1). The body "defends" itself against a decrease of weight or a limited supply of energy through a decreased metabolism. With more supply (three meals) the weight begins to increase slightly, because the metabolism has to catch up until a new balance is reached. The patients are therefore asked to weigh themselves at most once a week. For some this is no problem at all, because they are afraid of the confrontation with the scale. For others, this demands a serious effort because they weigh themselves up to 10 times a day.

> Angela, a 21-year-old saleswoman, started dieting 5 years ago. Very soon she discovered the way to vomit, and began to binge with all kinds of sweets. Because she still lives at home and does not want her parents to catch her vomiting, it often takes a lot of time before she can go outside the house to vomit. This made her weight increase considerably (36 lb) and for the last year she has been avoiding the scale. She now uses her clothing as a "standard."

> Petra, a 20-year-old student, has been struggling with bulimia for 3 years since going on a slimming diet. She studies at home, and her scale stands beside her desk. She weighs herself when getting up, after breakfast, before and after lunch, before and after supper,

after each bingeing cycle, and before going to bed. During exams, when she starts worrying about her weight, she weighs herself in order to reassure herself. In that way she attempts to maintain her ideal weight. Each increase in weight means eating less at the next meal. When her weight has remained unchanged after vomiting, she is reassured and does not have to give up bingeing, because she feels her weight to be under control.

Considering the sometimes violent emotional reactions to weight variations (which can lead to a binge), it may be wise in the initial phase to weigh the patients only during the session. This makes it possible to detect irrational thoughts about body shape and weight and to analyze these with the patient. The fundamental error made by these patients consists in trying to control at the same time both their eating behavior and their weight. This results mostly in an actual loss of control over both eating behavior and weight. Some BN patients show a slight overweight at the beginning of treatment, which disappears during the treatment. A minority show an obvious overweight (especially those who "cannot" purge). The urge for slenderness in this subgroup of patients can be interpreted as a desire for "normal" weight. Yet here too the priority remains the restoration of a sound eating pattern and certainly not a "new" diet. Another subgroup is formed by BN patients with an anorexic history. Their weight is usually too low at the beginning of the treatment. Normalization of the eating behavior will lead to the required increase in weight. Nevertheless, the anorexic nucleus can obstruct the restoration of the eating pattern. When it appears from the first agreements on the meals that this plays a part, arrangements must be made about weight restoration.

The structure of the *eating pattern* is laid out step by step, by making concrete agreements for each meal: time, place, quantity, and quality. Structuring the eating habits in space and time brings regularity necessary to restore the disturbed feeling of hunger and satiation. For the same reason, explicit agreements must be made on quantities. Patients often have no proper understanding of "normal" proportions in a meal, because they merely "weigh out" nourishment in calories, a habit they should quit. Counting calories of the binges can sometimes function to confront patients with the severity of the habit and the sharp contrast with the normally consumed food during the day. Because it is essential that patients should perceive an increased control over their eating behavior, agreements are made to prevent normal meals from resulting in binges: These meals should therefore not be vomited. If they cannot stand the urge to vomit, they should try to postpone it at least 30 minutes (and more, later on) so that food has the possibility to digest. Indeed, when patients allow themselves to vomit during the meal, they will be inclined to go on eating; in other words, the vomiting legitimates the binge and not vice versa, as many BN patients claim ("Help me to get rid of my binges, then I won't have to go on vomiting"). It could therefore be advisable for patients to avoid temporarily food that in itself elicits bingeing and vomiting. Still, it is quite a triumph for the patients to consume three meals daily, because this no longer means a diet for them. Thus they discover for the first time that the eating behavior can be controlled. The emphasis lies therefore in the first place on structure and regularity. The dietlike character of the meals can be reduced only by progressively enlarging the quantity on the one hand, and by breaking through the boundary between diet food and "forbidden" food on the other hand. The agreements on the two snacks are made in a similar way. We will illustrate this process of structuring a sound eating pattern by the example of Christine, whom we mentioned before (see "Case Example" below).

Apart from helping patients build up an eating pattern, the therapist should pay special attention to the way in which so many BN patients eat: quickly, greedily, swallowing everything without chewing or tasting what they eat. This does not alter the fact that for some the bingeing contains a rewarding or enjoyable aspect.

This way of eating thoroughly disturbs the feeling of hunger and satiation. In concrete steps we build up a sound and steady eating style so as to learn to respond to internal signals of hunger and satiation on the one hand, and on the other to learn again to eat heartily and to (dare) enjoy the food without any feelings of guilt (see Table 3).

A serious risk attached to this directive and structured approach is the fact that the agreements become a new control system with which patients can rigidly approach nourishment and weight. The fear of loss of control, an essential characteristic of BN, persists at the risk of later evolving toward an eating pattern of an anorexic nature. In order to overcome this fear it is necessary for patients to learn gradually to integrate "forbidden" and often binge-connected food into the meals and, later on, into the snacks. This exposure in vivo is gradually carried out by means of lists made

---

TABLE 3
Adaptation of Eating Style of BN Patients

Small quantities	Every time I eat, I take small bites in my mouth, which I can place under my tongue.
Eating slowly	I chew each bite 10 times, counting each chew in my mind according to the ticking of the seconds. I swallow only when the bite contains no more solid bits.
Tasting food	Each time, I taste a bite by pressing the chewed food on the palate with the tongue while making slight movements against the palate.
Pausing and relaxing	After having swallowed, I breathe a few times slowly and deeply. I put the next bite in my mouth only when the first one has been completely swallowed and after having breathed slowly and deeply.
Feeling satiation	As soon as I notice feelings of satiation and/or fatigue and/or the disappearance of the taste of the food, I finish eating and clear the table.

up by the patient (see "Case Example" below). This integration often takes a few months. Apart from this, it is also important that the patients gradually detach themselves from the previously fixed quantities in meals. This is connected with the acquisition of hunger and satiation feelings, which can sometimes take up to 6 months. As soon as patients succeed in basing themselves again on internal signals of hunger and satiation, they may determine the proportions of their meals by themselves. This will result in a well-balanced and varied eating pattern that does not cause guilt feelings and anxiety. The latter is connected with the most difficult step patients should make: learning to accept that their weight varies, both up and down, and that this is no longer a reflection of their feeling of self-esteem.

Intentionally, we have not presented in this part a survey of all possible self-control techniques. The choice of the different techniques and of the moment in which these are introduced depends on the functional analysis of the eating pattern of each patient and is also determined by the experience and creativeness of the therapist.

CONTROLLING THE BINGEING-VOMITING CYCLE

We have repeatedly emphasized that the purpose is a gradual self-control and not a drastic elimination of the binges. It is important that patients learn to discover the role of this bulimic behavior in their lives. The restoration of a sound and well-balanced eating pattern often has a twofold effect. The binges progressively decrease both in frequency and quantity because of patients' fear of becoming fat and because it is agreed that the binges may not replace normal meals. Because patients have to consume three meals, there is less "room" inside and, in the course of time, a lesser urge to binge.

Except for a few individual differences, the bingeing-vomiting cycles are brought under control as follows. The first step is the detailed charting of proportions and substance of the binge. The patients are expected to describe exactly what they eat and drink during a binge. This is the first necessary confrontation, because patients often refuse to know exactly how and what they binge. They often mix up their food without planning, and the binge ends when the stock is consumed. It is not unusual for them to perceive this situation as an outside power that dominates them (i.e., a dissociation feature, see Chapter 2). Keeping a diary sometimes stops them in the initial phase of a binge:

- "I have had fewer binges, for when I realized that I would have to write everything down, my urge was gone."
- "I have distracted my attention from the food, for I could not face the idea of writing everything down."

Sometimes the confrontation with the proportions can stop patients from continuing: "While keeping up how much I had been bingeing, I preferred to stop, for I thought it was horrible and it is senseless anyway." However, these effects are only temporary. The following steps are therefore necessary. The binges are structured in *space*: They take place only in an agreed-upon situation, in which it is not always possible to be alone. Thus, patients are also taught to control the urge when they do their shopping. Some start bingeing in the street or even in the store. The binges are also structured in *time*: Days and hours are fixed on when they may (but need not) binge. The frequency of these is decreased step by step. A list is made of alternative behaviors (such as taking a shower, calling up a friend, jogging) for whenever they have the urge to start bingeing outside the fixed times. This time planning necessitates well-structured and useful leisure activities in the moments that have become binge-free. Indeed, the leisure moments can be experienced as an emptiness or can cause boredom, which may lead to another binge.

The *content* of the binges can be structured step by step:

- Patients who still find themselves unable to store food in their houses can be told to make a list of foodstuffs that are bought solely for binges. This also permits the elaboration of a budget. After the purchases, everything is put on the table at home. Then they can start bingeing in a sitting position (and not walking around!). They are advised to make sufficient purchases to be "satiated," but the rest must be thrown in the garbage can.
- Families in which the bingeing behavior leads to tensions can be advised to have a special "binge cupboard." This is a cupboard in which a particular sort of food, in agreement with the patients (and the family), is stored. Whenever the patients feel the urge to binge, they will have to confine themselves to the content of the binge cupboard. The other family members are not allowed to use the cupboard. The stock in the cupboard must be sufficient. The patients can be asked to replenish and pay for stock themselves.
- The binge is restricted to one particular kind of preferred food, and after some time, to one particular unappealing sort of food (for instance, dried-out bread, beans).

The automatic bingeing-vomiting link is broken by the progressive delay of vomiting, so that this becomes "senseless" because the food is given time to be digested completely. In order to enhance the confrontation, patients are asked to vomit in a bucket, and not in the toilet anymore. The abuse of all sorts of laxatives and diuretics is also progressively reduced. The detachment from and the permanent stopping of these practices generally is accomplished more easily than the cessation of vomiting. This goes also for appetite suppressants. At any rate, possible abuse of other medicines (tranquilizers, sleeping pills) and alcohol should also be tackled.

Conclusion

The suggested approach has grown progressively within a behavior therapeutic framework in which the functional analysis of each patient's behavior forms a flexible guideline for the strategies to be used. Indeed, therapists too should beware of applying a rigid system of therapeutic techniques to restore the eating pattern. They have to accept that this restoration, during which dealing with relapses is an important skill, occurs slowly and laboriously. They should learn to accept that they may sometimes temporarily lose control over the course of the therapy. When patients learn to adopt a well-balanced eating pattern, the chances of a further favorable development of the therapy may increase. This means that they are prepared to work at their problems seriously and to make changes in their lives so that the bulimic behavior becomes superfluous.

The above described approach of the eating behavior is more than just "superficial symptom therapy." It brings about a radical change in the daily life of the patient and, via self-control, enhances the patient's self-esteem. It also offers the possibility (once the "escaping behavior" is under control) to include other problem areas in the therapy without again running the risk that each new conflict or frustration may result in binges. As soon as the circle is broken, there will be sufficient space and energy for more initiatives within and outside the therapy. Now therapy will shift to other focuses (the "real" issues), which may be handled according to various psychotherapeutic models. If possible, however, we prefer to continue therapy—phase 2—in the form of group therapy (see Chapter 5) and, if necessary, family or couple therapy (see Chapter 7). If things evolve unfavorably in the outpatient approach, a hospitalization might be the next step to consider (Chapter 8).

CASE EXAMPLE

In the case of Christine, as we mentioned earlier in this chapter, we illustrate the process of building up a sound eating pattern. This therapy runs over a period of 2 months with two sessions a week. It is a representative example of the step-by-step procedure and of the difficulties during this process that cause her to fall before standing up again. In the third session it is agreed with Christine to have a breakfast of a single sandwich with nonthreatening (no binge-provoking) filling at 7:45 A.M., after which she has to go to work immediately (i.e., refrain from bingeing). She carries on, but her responses betray the efforts she has to make:

> I can hardly stop. I feel like going on eating. The thought of having to wait till noon is dreadful. I am brooding over this one sandwich and I can hardly enjoy it. Eating is never enough, because I don't care what goes on in my stomach. The chewing gives me a sort of satisfaction and kind of numbs me. That's why I have to put off eating as much as possible, for when I taste the food I want to go on, and if I start bingeing in the morning, it lasts all day long. Then my weight is just ruined.

In the fifth session it is agreed to increase the quantity to two sandwiches, because she is now able to accept the breakfast. The fear of bingeing has lessened a little. In the sixth session it is decided that she should have a cold meal in a snackbar at noon, which should not induce her to binge. This means two bread rolls or one half French loaf or one piece of toast. She manages it, but then reports:

> Eating two sandwiches seems frightful to me, especially when I think that I have to stay inside all afternoon. I can't move enough that way, I have to be able to walk about. If I can't,

it looks like a punishment. The fear of the day makes me want to go on eating. To eat the day away.

In the next session it becomes clear that Christine spares herself no time. She "should" do all kinds of things. She also has to be physically active enough each day so as to keep her weight down. At noon she makes many roundabouts to go to a snackbar. At work she seizes any pretext to take the stairs. Only after 10 in the evening can she grant herself a rest in her apartment.

The following agreements are made:

1. To make a list of the activities she cannot carry out because of the urge to move (different leisure activities)
2. To stop walking around uselessly at work
3. To plan evening activities aimed at a balance between household activities and leisure activities she was unable to do
4. To go swimming for 1 hour per week (her list of wishes mentioned that she wanted to do something pleasant with her body in the way of sports)

From Christine's diary it appears that the changes in her eating and living patterns are still very unsteady after a month.

In the 10th session agreements are made also on two snacks. Times are fixed at 4:15 to 5:15 P.M. and 9:30 to 10:30 P.M. Christine is also asked to make lists of "forbidden" food that provokes anxiety, which will be included so as to eliminate the dietlike character of the meals.

Examples of sandwich filling:

Least anxiety: low-fat cheese spread, low-fat soft cheese, ham, roast beef, turkey or chicken breast, veal

A *little anxiety*: pork, jam, ground steak, smoked ham, all sorts of cheese, filleted herrings

Extreme anxiety: salami, chocolate, all salads with mayonnaise, all

Christine's Diary

Time	Consumed Food, Drinks	Place	V/L	Context (activities, feelings, and thoughts)	
				Before	After
9:00 A.M.	2 sandwiches with cheese spread	Car		The reason why I ate in the car this morning is that I had to rush to the doctor for a blood sample. I managed not to move around all night. I haven't left the classroom from 9:15 to 12:30, except for once, to discuss something urgent with a colleague. However, I am glad it's Monday and to be in a familiar surrounding again where there is less tension than at home.	
12:45 P.M.	2 slices of bread and ham, 1 coffee	Pub		There is one danger to the increase of the number of meals—that I may be inclined to refuse	

Time	Food	Location	Thoughts / Feelings
	eating again, to bring it down in other moments. How is it then, that it has been quite a while since I last felt this uncontrollable urge to abandon everything and go eat?		This scares me. Moreover, I feel very swollen now.
7:00 P.M.	1 plate of soup, 1 portion of carrots stewed in some butter, 1 slice of bread with (low-fat) liver paste, 1 large slice of bread with a little butter, and 1 big slice of cheese	Living room	
10:00 P.M.			The reason why I start panicking is that if I eat normally at normal times with normal ends, I have to find something else important enough to live for, something different

Continued . . .

from those good sandwiches in the evening. I went to the sewing lesson, I'm just back. It is a strange experience, a new experience, to go somewhere with a stomach that feels full of me, without coming back with the prospect: Now I can start eating. There is an important difference to me between giving up complete abstinence during the day and trying to say no to my urge on the one hand, and giving up eating late in the evening in the other. In the first case I did it for myself because both fasting during the day and the urge to move, as well as the frequent vomiting, are things that make me cause myself pain. The circumstances were safe enough to dare give up those things and get something better in return, which no longer causes me pain.

| 10:25 P.M. | 1 portion of soft cheese, 1 big sandwich with cheese and jam, 1 slice of raisen bread | Living room |
| 11:15 P.M. | 2 slices of gingerbread | |

fat sorts of meat such as sausages, liver paste, currant or sugar bread with butter

In the following sessions, it is agreed that Christine will eat one sandwich with filling of the category "a little anxiety" at supper. In addition, the quantities of bread meals are increased from two to three sandwiches in the morning and three to four sandwiches in the evening. Meanwhile, her weight has decreased to within the normal bounds and she has one to three binges a week. Since these can sometimes thoroughly disturb the agreements of the day, Christine then has the feeling that she has failed all along the line. During these sessions we explain that these binges are a signal that certain things in her life go wrong. Together we will try to discover their significance. Thus, the binge will no longer be an enemy that must be fought, but an ally trying to make something clear to her. She is taught to put the disturbed eating behavior in a wider context, and depth is given to the content of the problem areas that will have to be worked on in due time.

In the 13th session, after a weekend, Christine throws her diary on the table, saying that she has messed up everything—"The weekend has been a complete mess"—and she starts crying. She has had five binges, which has never happened since the therapy started. Because of this, her Sunday's eating scheme had been completely messed up. Yet the other days she did keep to the agreements. From a closer analysis of the weekend, it appears that she had done everything that her friend William had suggested. She did not dare to suggest initiatives she knew he would not appreciate. The only way to oppose this was to start bingeing. Together we check out what she would like to do next weekend. She will discuss this with William during the week, so that next weekend some things she likes may be done as well. Without dramatization, the mistakes are analyzed as a function of the agreements that have been made. Once again, the importance of continuing to try eating "forbidden food" is emphasized. All agreements appear to be feasible, so that she can leave the session full of hope again: "If I could make it before everything went wrong on the weekend, I can make it this time as well."

In the 14th session, it is decided to make agreements on the binges. After having mutually considered the feasibility, we made the following agreements:

1. Binges may take place exclusively between 10:30 and 11:30 P.M.; it is permitted to binge every day.
2. The procedure we work out is the "binge bag": She will buy any food she wants to eat for about $20, which she will put in a bag in the trunk of her car. When it is "binge time" she is allowed to get the bag out of the car and to start bingeing. What is left of the bag will be thrown into the garbage can. The next day, another bag will be bought so that a binge bag is always available each day.
3. No laxatives will be taken.
4. No alcohol will be consumed during the binge.
5. Vomiting will be allowed 15 minutes after bingeing.

Although Christine feared that these agreements would make her binge each day—since it is allowed—this has, to her own amazement, the opposite effect. She is now made responsible for consciously deciding whether she will binge or not. This consciousness often makes her choose alternatives from her list.

Yet the agreements present her with a problem. She sometimes feels like eating something from the binge bag during a meal or snack, and at times she does not feel like bingeing at all. But when she seizes her binge bag, she thinks, "I may as well eat everything," and so she starts on a binge again! It is then agreed to store more forbidden food in the house. Her weight remains within the agreed bounds, and she is asked to weigh herself only one morning in a week.

After 2 months, we decide to proceed to phase 2, group therapy, while in parallel a few complementary individual sessions are planned, but more widely spaced in time, to continue the achieved changes and to further bring under control the bingeing-vomiting cycles. After this sketch by the therapist, here is Christine's account, as she looks back on the first 2 months of her therapy.

The most amazing thing to me is—still now—the speed with which I succeeded in building up a fairly regular eating pattern in the therapy. Whereas I have been living for 10 years in a rhythm of fasting during the day and bingeing in the evening, and later of bingeing and vomiting, I have succeeded, in something over 8 weeks, in building up an eating scheme of three meals and two snacks, and in continuing to do so (more or less) without frequent binges and also in spite of occasional binges. Initially, this was one of the most difficult things: to keep to this eating scheme—especially after a binge. Indeed, after a binge I used to fast for 24 hours, and the idea of having breakfast after a night binge seemed insuperable to me.

It was and still is very difficult to follow the complete eating scheme on the day after a binge. Then I start panicking about putting on weight again. At first, the agreements looked very compelling to me: You have to have your breakfast, even if you had a binge the night before; you have to have two slices of bread for breakfast; you have to eat at noon, even if you have been moving very little in the morning or just been sitting in a chair. . . . Later on, they looked rather freeing to me: I can have breakfast each morning, something I did not allow myself to do; I mustn't use stairs uselessly; I can sit still on a chair for quite a while . . .

For me, increasing quantities is more difficult than building up a regularity. One bread roll or one biscuit at noon seemed feasible, but doubling it looked insuperable. I remember my first panicking when I ordered a French loaf. Even now, after 4 months, the trickiest thing for me is not to fall back on minimum quantities, rather than skipping meals.

The agreements about bingeing (a bingeing time and a binge bag) roused and still arouse ambivalent feelings in me. On the other hand, they can also be relieving, especially the installation of the binge bag. In that way, the food stays in my fridge. I don't have to store masses of quantities for normal meals either. Besides, a binge bag nearly always contains the same thing, so that I no longer have to walk around for hours in the supermarket to decide what to binge. Hoarding up food from the binge bag in the house is dangerous, even now. I am still very afraid to eat a sugar waffle, for fear of devouring the whole pack. I also find it hard to switch over to a binge bag containing just one kind of food, because then I often feel like bingeing with other food than just cakes. Placing the bingeing time between 10:30 and 11:30 P.M. has certainly checked a number of binges, though it may sometimes be hard to keep it up till 10:30. On the other hand, I feel so guilty whenever I have exceeded the time or the content. However, it was very important for me to have been able to trust you and the therapy. It seemed safe enough to take chances, and it could not run completely out of hand (because of the two sessions per week, and the possibility to call if there were any problems—however difficult the latter was and still is). I am convinced of the fact that this would have been impossible a few years ago, that I would have known better at that time, and that I wouldn't have dared to lend myself to any agreements about food.

5

Group Therapy

This chapter reflects 10 years of clinical experience with group therapy in about 250 BN patients. The majority of these patients had had inpatient treatment in a specialized group-therapeutic program (see Chapter 8) and subsequently were incorporated into outpatient group therapy (we call this group A). In addition to this, we have had experience with "pure" outpatient group therapy in more than 80 BN patients who had not yet had inpatient treatment (group B). This approach has grown from the experience that in severe cases even intensive individual therapy (twice a week) had little effect on certain aspects of the BN issue, such as the preoccupation with food and weight, the impaired self-esteem, and the detection and exploration of the signaling function of the binges. The experiences with both groups run mostly parallel. If there are apparent differences in the operating procedure of the groups, we shall mention them hereafter.

GENERAL CHARACTERISTICS

Each week one group therapy session takes place during 1½ hours. In crisis situations patients can request an individual session, but this occurs very rarely. Group A is composed of BN patients who had previously had inpatient treatment in our center. Hence, these patients are already acquainted with group therapy. Group B is composed of BN patients who have made sufficient progress during previous individual therapy (see Chapter 4). The restriction of the group size to a maximum of six patients is aimed at keeping under control flight attempts and escaping maneuvers, and at enlarging the possibility of active participation. Agreements are made beforehand with each patient in the form of a contract, signed by both patient and therapist (see Appendix D). The majority of these patients are in the age group of 20 to 30 years. Thus, most BN patients find themselves at the launching stage in their life cycle (departure from parental environment). Many already live on their own or with a partner, which does not mean that they are emotionally detached from their parents.

Our approach is to be regarded as a form of directive therapy (Vandereycken et al., 1986):

- The group therapy is rather *pragmatically* oriented; it is meant to achieve well-defined therapeutic goals within a particular lapse of time.
- The therapy is *eclectically* inspired; the approach contains, among others, behavioral, cognitive, and interactional components (sometimes hypnotic techniques are also included in the therapeutic repertoire).
- Explicit use is made of *nonspecific* therapy factors, such as building up a good work relationship, in which both the authority of the therapist and the creation of hope and positive expectations are used consciously and purposely.
- The directive approach necessitates an *active participation* of both patient and therapist.

BN is considered as a signal or expression that something serious is wrong in the patient's private life, partner relationship, and/or family context. In that sense our treatment is not exclusively focused on the control or elimination of the symptomatic behavior ("bulimia") but should certainly pay as much attention to its meaning and function (the element "nervosa"). This means that it aims at rendering the symptomatic behavior superfluous.

SPECIFIC THERAPEUTIC STRATEGIES

Hereafter we shall give a survey of the principal strategies and interventions in our group-therapeutic approach to BN. This is but a sketch of the main ingredients in which the emphasis varies according to the patient.

Goal Attainment Evaluation (GAE)

We developed a specific therapy-oriented assessment procedure, which is employed in both inpatient and outpatient treatments (see Appendix B). Each patient is expected to identify problem areas on three levels (symptoms, self-perception, interactions) and to determine for each problem area concrete steps as a short-term objective. This is illustrated by the following example (we confine ourselves to one problem per category).

A. *Symptom*: I still vomit after each meal.

Step a— Resume work immediately after each meal.

Step b— If very difficult, listen to hypnosis tape.

Step c— Call up my friend.

B. *Self-perception*: My body disgusts me.

Step a— Use some makeup each day.

Step b— Buy a new article of clothing.

Step c— Go swimming twice a week.

C. *Interactions*: I have neither boyfriends nor girlfriends.

Step a— Invite my old school friend to do something.

Step b— Join a volleyball club.

Step c— Put an advertisement in a local newspaper.

At fixed times (every 3 months), follows an evaluation session in which treatment objectives are assessed and, if needed, adjusted. The GAE form functions as a guideline for outlining the treatment strategy.

Diary

The diary is also a crucial element in group therapy. Patients are expected (as agreed upon in the treatment contract) to keep a detailed diary in which they will write down their daily eating pattern, activities, and accompanying thoughts and feelings. In order to facilitate and structure this task, a standard form has been designed (see Chapter 4, pp. 63–65). The patients are expected to send the diary to the group therapist a few days before the session, so that the therapist may read it in advance.

In this way, the therapist is given a lot of information in a short time, not only on the eating behavior and the context in which possible binges take place, but especially on accompanying thoughts, beliefs, and feelings of the patients. The diary not only provides a great deal of input for the therapy sessions, but also gives the therapist immediate feedback on the impact of the therapeutic strategies. At the beginning of the session, the therapist briefly discusses each diary and mentions the principal events and elements.

From Annette's diary, the therapist gathers that she felt very tired, lifeless, and anxiety-ridden during the past week. She binged three times but managed not to vomit afterward. She also rejected her boyfriend whenever he approached her to make love. He had hardly paid any attention to her physical looks. The discussion of this relapse—which was mentioned immediately through the diary—reveals that Annette had been very afraid of the expected visit of her parents and grandmother. This would be the first visit (control?) since she had started to live with her boyfriend—very much against the wishes of her parents and especially her grandmother. This planned visit again gave her strong feelings of guilt about her living together with her boyfriend, which was signaled by the bulimia.

Whether this is discussed in depth during the session is the responsibility of the patient herself: It is up to her to decide whether she wishes to continue working on this particular subject or not. This implies a confrontation with a potential escape route. Certain patients explicitly ask not to discuss in the group what they write in their diaries. In that way, they test the reliability of the therapist. The latter then risks being allied with one group member. It is therefore necessary that the request for secrecy should be discussed in the group, respecting the privacy of the patient by not discussing the content of the theme if the patient requests this explicitly.

Self-Control

The general goal in the beginning is to reach a better control of the eating pattern and to reduce step by step the binge-purge behavior. As mentioned before, it is advisable not to advance total abstinence (i.e., complete and permanent cessation of bingeing and vomiting) as an essential or primary objective. This "take it or leave it" rule would only be a repetition of what these patients have been striving after for years in vain. In a predictable relapse (which frequently occurs) this will contribute to the patient's feeling of insufficiency and inferiority. Instead, patients should be prepared to deal with relapses. The binges are looked upon as an ally capable of making them understand that something goes wrong in their lives. In order to enhance the control of the eating pattern, we use self-control and stimulus control procedures (see Chapter 4). The patient is expected to analyze in detail the stimulus-response chain (mostly loneliness, restlessness, or tension followed by bingeing and vomiting). We must look for the weak link in order to intervene, if needed, in the series of thoughts, behaviors, and feelings that lead to bingeing and vomiting. At the same time, alternative behavior for bingeing and vomiting should be programmed and taught.

When the binges lessen effectively, patients can buy themselves something nice with the money that would have been spent on binges. This must be inquired about with insistence, because the patients are not used to buying things for themselves, apart from binge food. Although it is a general rule that the people in the immediate environment (parents, partner, etc.) shall not interfere with the eating behavior of the patient, we may in particular cases appeal to their assistance. It can be agreed, for instance, that the parents will temporarily lock off the kitchen at night, strictly restrict the food stocks at home, and remove pocket money for the time being (see Chapter 7). Sometimes the boundaries between the patient and the other family members can be better marked out by using the "binge cupboard" (see Chapter 4, p.77).

Cognitive Restructuring

The diary is an especially useful instrument to trace irrational conceptions and ideas of BN patients. They are encouraged to identify any ideas that may hamper possible change. Such black-and-white and all-or-none reasonings frequently occur in BN patients:

- "When I start eating, I just can't stop."
- "After each meal I feel as fat as an elephant."
- "I have to do everything exactly as I plan."
- "It has to be perfect, or else I feel like a failure."
- "Nobody is interested in me."

They are combined with an extreme achievement orientation and perfectionist attitude, which repeatedly make these patients feel like failures. The group-therapeutic situation lends itself very well to their replacing this negative way of reasoning and perceiving themselves with more realistic and constructive thoughts and perceptions. Again and again, we are struck in the group sessions by the rather negative way in which patients perceive and evaluate themselves. In order to correct this negative line of reasoning, the group members are asked to note all positive qualities about a fellow patient on a paper. The patient is to take this paper home and hang it up in the bedroom. During this exercise we notice that many group members feel uneasy or tense. Appreciating oneself and learning to recognize one's own qualities is a difficult task for many of them.

Exploring the Bulimic Message

In group therapy patients learn to examine, together with the other group members, the function and meaning of the bulimia in their private life, family system, or marital relationship. The patients are invited to "listen" to unexpressed wishes and feelings. Bulimia is then regarded as a messenger of all kinds of frustrations, anxiety, and desires. Before trying to alter the bulimia, one should try to decode the message or hidden meaning of the bulimic symptoms. One can discover the hidden significance by asking patients to write down both the advantages and the disadvantages of effective change and to discuss them in the group therapy (see Chapter 4).

It is not unusual for patients to discover that the bulimia functions as a lightning conductor for tensions between parents or for unexpressed conflicts in the marital relationship. Once there exists a trustful atmosphere, it is remarkable how openly patients first start discussing family or marital problems in the group sessions. Patients are often more accessible to confrontation and explanation from other group members than from the therapist.

> Joan has been married for 10 months. Remarkably enough, she started bingeing and vomiting in that time. When the therapist

carefully asks her if there might be a connection between her marriage and the bingeing, she immediately and strongly rejects this assumption. Catherine then tells the story of her feeling like a stranger at home, misunderstood by her husband, who just let everything happen and never even interfered with her bingeing. In addition, when she tells how bad or absent their sexual relationship was, Joan suddenly becomes very tense and sad. She starts crying and tells how many similarities she sees with her own marriage.

Moreover, patients dare to confront each other directly with flight attempts, in sometimes tough terms a therapist would never dare to use. In this way, preparations are made in the group session for themes that can be further explored later on in the partner, couple, or family therapy.

Whenever Eliza goes home on the weekend, she finds it hard to keep her eating behavior under control, whereas during the week she hardly has any difficulties in her room. When the therapist points out that this might have something to do with the bad relationship between her parents, she denies this. Martine, who has had to detach herself from the perils of her parents' divorce, replies: "You simply don't want to face the possibility of your parents' separation. And you can't do anything about that. It's their business and you must live your own life." Eliza looks down at the floor in dejection and nods yes.

In patients who experience the bulimia as something strange, as if someone else dominated them during the binge—a sort of dissociated state—attempts can be made in a *role play* to get in touch with the "bulimic part" (see also Chapter 6). Such a role play, which often arouses violent emotions and therefore must be prepared with caution, runs as follows: The patient is asked to carry on a dialogue with another group member who is identified with "the bulimia." It is remarkable how smoothly most patients can play this bulimic role. Sometimes we ask the patient to carry on the dialogue between the two parts alone. Then the patient will be invited to take a place alternatingly on two chairs: the bulimic chair and the often perfectionistic opposite chair. The patient is then asked to sit on one chair and talk to the opposite chair, and then reverse roles.

> Louise, a 24-year-old BN patient, is quite willing to get more closely acquainted with the "bulimic part" within her. She will play the role of the person who keeps fighting against the abominable and all-destroying bulimia. In addition, she is very demanding and perfectionistic. Another group member, Sue, is willing to play the role of the abominable bulimia. The role play runs as follows:

> *Louise:* Why can't you vanish from my life once and for all? I hate you, why are you always pestering me?
> *Sue:* You have never even accepted me, you are always pushing me away. The only way for me to come into your life is bingeing and vomiting.
> *Louise:* Who are you anyway?
> *Sue:* I feel weak, frightened, lonely, and empty. And you keep pushing me away, you never allow me to take up a place in your life. You are always so exacting.
> After that, Louise starts crying very emotionally.

The purpose of this role play is the creation of a contact and dialogue between "parts of the self," often two extremes, which we try to bring more closely together, to reconcile with one another. Such a role play is recognizable for nearly all patients, namely the splitting up between two extremes: a perfectionist, demanding attitude on the one hand and a weak, empty, and anxious part on the other.

Alternating Between Direct and Indirect Strategies

Self-control procedures, meant to teach patients to acquire more direct control of their eating pattern, are usually alternated with more indirect, resistance-detouring techniques. The group therapist might in the latter case display a skeptical attitude and ask the patient or the group as a whole if they are indeed ready to abandon their symptoms and make choices for a fundamental change in their life. In those moments the therapist reflects the ambivalent attitude of the BN patient in regard to a radical change, and all patients are invited to consider both the positive and the negative consequences of abandoning the symptoms. The therapist no longer emphasizes the fight against the bulimia and the accompanying (depressive) feelings. Instead of patients constantly trying to push away the most depressive feelings, they are told that these have a significant signaling function. Feelings of sadness should be taken seriously and analyzed at fixed times (for instance, through a diary), in order to uncover how it is that one feels so miserable, sad, or empty. The bulimia and the depression then become a means to achieve better self-knowledge and change. This attitude also goes straight against the "ban" on the expression of feelings (both positive and negative) that is often deeply ingrained in these families (see Chapter 7).

Encouraged by a few enthusiastic reports on the use of *hypnosis* in BN patients (see Chapter 6), we have in turn introduced hypnotic techniques into the group therapy. Considering the group situation, we exclusively use supporting, relaxing, and ego-strengthening techniques, whereas exploring techniques (for instance ego state, affect bridge) are avoided. Self-hypnosis techniques and guided-fantasy exercises are used in order for patients to learn to relax in the situation at home (with use of an audiotape). Moreover, hypnotic techniques are used to teach self-control methods; in the process patients may be asked to imagine a threatening situation without giving way to a binge. During the hypnosis exercises positive suggestions (i.e., ego-strengthening suggestions), are regularly given, so that patients will feel gradually better and satisfied in their body and, in the course of time, learn to adopt a more independent attitude. Through future-directed fantasy exercises, patients learn to imagine a life without bulimia and to consider all positive changes that the cessation of the binges may bring about.

Teaching Specific Skills

Inspired by social skills training programs, we devote a monthly session to the teaching and practicing through role plays of one specific new skill: self-assertion, expression of anger, opposing others, learning to express feelings, and expressing and responding to affection. Most patients apparently lack assertiveness: Responses are either subassertive or too aggressive. By mutual arrangement with the group members, one specific skill is chosen and, subsequently, different concrete situations are practiced through role playing. At the end of the session, the different group members are given specific tasks in order to continue practicing and trying out these skills outside of the therapy.

> Marianne dares not tell her parents that she does not like the idea of spending each weekend with them. She now lives on her own and would like to spend a weekend with her friend. The skill of self-assertion is chosen from this situation, since other group members recognize similar situations. The role play appears to have been an excellent preparation to talking over this problem directly with Marianne's parents in the family session.

THE THERAPEUTIC PROCESS

As for the group therapy process, we can distinguish different phases (see Figure 3), which all include a few specific pitfalls. In practice there exists a constant fluctuation between the different phases. In the following chapters on hypnotherapy and family therapy, also, a similar therapeutic process can be discerned.

When BN patients find themselves in the outpatient group therapy, after having first been treated individually or on an inpatient unit, they are mostly in phase 3, wherein stimulating and encouraging independence are central. The discharge from the hospital means for many the first step toward living independently. This is often accompanied by a temporary relapse into the well-known symptomatology and, therefore, a regression into a previous treatment phase. Also, the transition from individual therapy to group

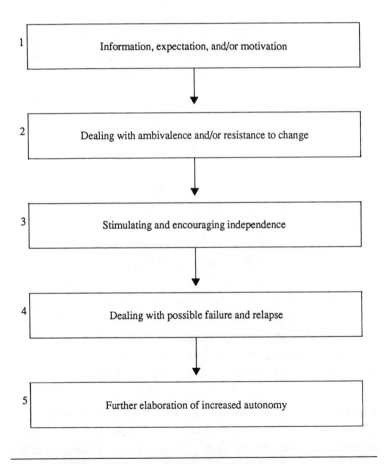

Figure 3. Different Phases in the Therapeutic Process.

therapy in an outpatient setting is often accompanied by a relapse, which is predicted by the therapist. Patients are now confronted with others with similar problems, and they have to share the attention of the therapist, which sometimes makes them feel abandoned. Initially, especially in group B, this caused several dropouts in the group. It was then decided to make use of a transitional phase in which individual sessions would be combined with group sessions. Roughly, BN patients seem to go through the following steps, both in inpatient and outpatient treatment.

In a first phase, the therapist will mainly *provide information* on the gravity, persistence, and physical complications of bingeing and vomiting. If possible, the family (parents, partner) will be actively involved in this phase (see Chapter 7). When one decides to commit oneself to the treatment, the treatment should have absolute priority in one's life. Once the therapy has started, every possible kind of help and solution is expected from the expert. The therapist may then be tempted to offer direct solutions. Whoever promptly suggests such a direct approach risks being as promptly disillusioned by a "passive sabotage" of the suggested directives.

In order to avoid this pitfall, we first try to *confront patients with their ambivalence and/or resistance to change.* The therapist then rather adopts a skeptical and expectant attitude, asking patients whether they are ready to give absolute priority to the treatment. When the patients (and possibly family members or partner) become gradually aware of the function of the symptomatology in their private lives, *promoting and encouraging independence* will take up a central place in the treatment. Significant themes in the group sessions will be the working through of the emotional dependence and loyalty in regard to the family of origin and, eventually, the negotiations about living independently. The group therapist should pay full attention to this separation issue. The group then often gains the status of a sort of foster family wherein group members encourage and challenge each other to make the step toward an independent life. But group members can become too dependent on one another as well!

The separation-individuation issue provokes in many patients a temporary relapse into the bulimic symptomatology. The therapist should therefore *prepare* both patient and family (partner) *for this possible relapse.* Frequent themes then are the perfectionist attitude; dealing with feelings of emptiness and abandonment (in connection with independent life and social isolation); fear of new peer contacts and sexuality; feelings of loyalty in regard to the family of origin; the expression of aggressive feelings; and working through traumatic experiences.

Every month an evaluation takes place in which the patients evaluate the progress made in the past period (with GAE form). The continuation or termination of treatment will also be discussed. We have learned that psychotherapy in BN patients is lengthy and that short-term effects of the treatment can hardly guarantee a favorable evolution in the future. In certain cases we decide for ourselves to stop a treatment when the patient continually keeps sabotaging (often in a passive way) the treatment, which is in the end very harmful to a favorable group-therapeutic climate. Indeed, a real pitfall is that patients use the group therapy to confirm their identity as chronic and incurable patient and/or to give their family a pretended reassurance by staying in a pseudotreatment, rather than to change actually. Another danger is to be found in a sort of negative mutual competition, as in, "Who is worst off?" It is absolutely necessary to detect and discuss these group interactions (often repetitions of family interactions) in due time.

Sylvia, a 28-year-old bulimic patient, is always late for the session but time after time dares to ask for a lot of attention by telling at great length how bad she feels and how worthless the treatment is. As a result of this attitude, most group members get more and more annoyed by her. Sylvia grows conscious of this and once again has it confirmed for herself that nobody in this group cares about her. She used to have the same feeling with her family at home.

The group points out the similarity between the group and the family situations, and they discuss the ever-recurring scenario: Sylvia draws attention via her complaints, but at the same time, she rejects all help and support of the others. In that way, she always achieves her own isolation. This repeats itself in the group. After this session Sylvia becomes genuinely involved in treatment.

In cases of favorable evolution, patients may reduce the frequency of group sessions (every 2 weeks instead of every week) and thus gradually reduce group contact. In group B (a "closed" group) the frequency of group sessions is not reduced: When sufficient progress appears to have been made, and the group is no longer needed, the group therapy is stopped and the aftercare is again provided on an individual basis, with time between sessions being lengthened progressively (see Chapter 9).

Final Considerations

The group approach is an interesting one, both from economical and therapeutic points of view. In the group, BN patients appear to abandon the well-known defense mechanisms and resistances much sooner, and manage to explore their symptomatology more directly and thoroughly on a psychological level. Chapter 9 contains an evaluation of our experiences with this approach. When we compare our preliminary results to follow-up data of other researchers (e.g., Fairburn, 1985; Lacey, 1983) we sometimes feel frustrated. Are other therapists really that much better? Or are we treating different patients? From our many years of experience in the treatment of eating disorder patients, we have learned one thing for sure: The issue is very complex and requires a multidimensional and long-lasting approach. It would be naive and therapeutically dangerous to expect BN patients to achieve a fundamental change (on both symptomatic and psychosocial, individual and interactional levels) after some 10 therapeutic sessions. Patience, perseverance, realism, and flexibility not only should be expected from patients, they should also be among the skills of each therapist.

CASE EXAMPLE

Louise is a 24-year-old student who contacts us spontaneously because of a totally uncontrollable bulimia, always followed by vomiting and/or abuse of laxatives. At the same time Louise regularly feels badly depressed, has serious suicidal thoughts, and roams around the town for hours on end. She often drinks too much alcohol and has "a smoke" to make herself feel better; or she seeks comfort in lovemaking with a boyfriend. Recently Louise has felt more and more anxious and tense. "I can't sit still for a minute," she tells us. She has lost all concentration and can no longer study. This makes her feel even worse and leads to bingeing, drinking, and so on. Finally, she plucks up her courage and calls for help for the first time. She has been in trouble for about 10 years!

Background Data

Before discussing Louise's evolution in group therapy, we will mention a few important background data. Louise's childhood and youth were shadowed by serious conflicts between her parents. Her mother went through a few psychotic phases, for which psychiatric help was sought. When Louise was 13, her parents divorced and each started a new relationship. Louise then was confronted with a serious loyalty problem: She was given the choice of which parent she wanted to live with. Around that time she started bingeing and vomiting secretly. She chose her father, but later on she felt guilty and went to live with her mother again. She felt herself swing between both parents and was also assigned the responsibility for the education of her two younger sisters. They lived with her father, who had meanwhile become very depressed. Both sisters were regularly truant, drank too much alcohol, and went through "very hard times." Louise never talked to anybody about her problems. After high school she decided to live in a room, hoping that the change of environment might solve her problem. Things were better at first, but gradually the bulimia increased again, and finally she called for therapeutic help. Considering the complexity of the problem (diagnosed as multisymptomatic bulimia with depression, danger of suicide, alcohol abuse, sexual promiscuity), Louise is referred to the inpatient treatment (for a description of the therapeutic program, see Chapter 8). In the following section we shall give a survey of the therapeutic process that Louise went through in group therapy and which elements and strategies played an important role in her treatment.

Therapeutic Process

It takes several weeks before Louise manages to fill out her Goal Attainment Evaluation (GAE) form. Initially, she finds it very hard to admit that she has problems. In the group, she is quiet and keeps in the background. Moreover, she wants a perfect GAE: She is afraid that her objectives may not be appreciated. Finally, she writes down the following.

A. *Symptoms*

*Problem area 1: I still have a bulimic urge each day, feelings and things I cannot cope with; spitting them out gives me a feeling of relief.

    Step a— Reflect on the bulimic urge and try to find out its cause.

    Step b— Recognize that I have certain feelings and possibly communicate them to others.

    Step c— Find out a different way to express feelings.

*Problem area 2: I still have problems with some foods because they call up certain memories.

Step a— Try to better appreciate the taste of that food.
Step b— Try to put aside the memories of the past.
Step c— If I fail, talk about it afterward.

B. *Self-perception*

*Problem area 1: Tensions always refer to my (swollen) belly; problems with clothing: I can still not wear anything fitted at the waist.

Step a— Try to find out why I am tense.
Step b— Learn to be more peaceful through breathing and relaxation exercises.
Step c— Try not to always conceal my belly, though it bulges.

*Problem area 2: When I feel lousy I start doing all kinds of things and I am restless; when I keep calm "everything" comes up.

Step a— Let the other group members tell me when I'm running around again.
Step b— Try to admit to myself that there is something wrong when I feel so overexcited.
Step c— Try consciously to do nothing or simply sit still knitting or reading.

C. *Interactions*

*Problem area 1: I try to be strong, dare not show that I am weak (consciously or not); I dare not say anything when I am worried about something and what I am worried about.

Step a— Note thoughts and feelings.
Step b— Talk to someone about rotten feelings.
Step c— Dare to talk in the group about the things that keep me preoccupied.

*Problem area 2: I am often cynical with men, as a sort of self-protection; I then seem cold and hard, whereas in fact I feel exactly the opposite.

Step a— Reflect on the reason for my cynicism and then admit
it to myself.

Step b— Try not to translate feelings of grief, disappointment,
and humiliation into aggression/rage.

Step c— Try not to avoid the persons concerned but instead,
talk to them about those feelings.

The discussion of these objectives in the group sessions is a difficult step for Louise. She expects the group members to find her
treatment plan ridiculous or to disapprove of it, and she is therefore
extremely tense. After the discussion of her objectives, Louise
becomes silent again in the group during the following weeks. She
finds it hard to accept that she is under treatment and has a lot
of criticism of the system in the hospital. The eating symptoms
come somewhat to the front again. She has difficulty in keeping
to normal portions, eats in a very forced way, again feels a bulimic
urge, and can accept her target weight only with difficulty. Louise
has come to know that the bulimic urge has a signaling function,
but she is afraid to explore its significance in group therapy. It is
agreed in the team not to confront her too strongly, not to insist
but to respect her own rhythm. Indeed, in a too-strong confrontation she threatens to be overwhelmed by anxiety and depressive
feelings, with the risk of a flight out of the hospital.

After about 6 weeks' stay in the group, we notice that she finds
it harder to conceal her feelings. She is very afraid to show her weakness: "It makes you vulnerable and people will cause you a lot of
pain," she says. She is told in the group therapy that "you are strong
only when you dare to show your weaknesses." Louise now becomes
sad; she cries for hours on end and feels suicidal. In the group therapy she begins to talk carefully about her depression and bulimic
urges. She is now ready to explore this and tells about a series of
nasty and sad experiences: infernal quarrels between her parents,
her mother being overstrained, her own loneliness and helplessness,

the loyalty conflicts (the fear of being unable to make the right choice, of either father or mother). From this grew a deep-rooted conviction: "No one takes me seriously, you can't trust anyone." Bingeing and vomiting are the only means to make herself feel peaceful in that situation. Later on, Louise finds out that her bingeing and vomiting are also a way to express her intense anger with her parents (especially her father), in particular, her feelings of having been misused in the marital conflicts.

Four months later, the group concludes her third evaluation as follows: "Louise, you are now able to admit that you are always very busy and you also do something about it (for instance, talking about it). You no longer repress your feelings, and we also notice that you express deeper feelings. Try to find some consistency in this, so that it may not remain a big chaos of feelings and memories." As soon as Louise abandons her forced facade and begins to express her feelings, she grows anxious and tense. Physically, a significant change comes about: She begins menstruating spontaneously again and is very glad about this. This apparently also removes a blockade. However, sadness continues to exist for several weeks. It appears that she is going through a kind of mourning process with frequent fits of crying and hopelessness. However, the group members support her and encourage her. Gradually, Louise gets the feeling that she has thrown off a large part of the burden of the past, and her planning of the future comes more to the front. This results in *new treatment objectives* (after about 4½ months of inpatient treatment). Remarkably enough, the eating problems are now completely in the background, whereas self-perception and interactions now take up a central place.

A. *Eating problems*

*Problem area 1: Too much and irregular coffee drinking.
   Step a— Drink one cup (maximum two) at fixed times only.
   Step b— Drink more water in between.

*Problem area 2: Frequent nibbling between meals, especially fruit.

Step a— Fix a certain quantity of food per day.

Step b— Eat fruit at fixed times only.

B. *Self-perception*

*Problem area 1: I have problems with my lack of self-confidence; I am afraid to fall into the other extreme of what I thought I was: dependent, devoted, clumsy.

Step a— Accept feelings of uncertainty, and not regard nerv-ousness as shameful.

Step b— Do things I have to do by small steps.

Step c— Be myself in all circumstances and no longer put on that mask.

*Problem area 2: I feel much empathy for other people, and I feel too responsible for them; I would also like to be able to listen to my own feelings, to stand up for myself, but I often try to avoid such situations.

Step a— Avoid no confrontation, for example, by backing out of the group.

Step b— Say what I feel whenever I have a problem.

Step c— Find a compromise and put up with it, though I don't quite like the idea.

C. *Interactions*

*Problem area 1: I feel like a burden, a failure to my father; I find it hard to ask him for help (for example, money, moving).

Step a— Talk to Father about those feelings.

Step b— Talk about finances in time and show everything in black and white.

Step c— Ask for other people's help whenever possible.

*Problem area 2: I find it hard to make new contacts (in which way?); I have the impression that everyone can see that I am so uncertain and that I have been bulimic.

Step a— Try not to feel sorry for myself.
Step b— Openly admit my uncertainty.
Step c— Simply talk about my interests and plans for the
 future.

In the last period of the treatment, when the bulimia and vomiting are overcome, Louise has the feeling of going through a sort
of identity crisis, as if she is becoming a "different person," someone
she does not want to be. At times she feels empty. In the group
therapy, she is strongly encouraged to make a realistic plan for the
future: By planning new activities she can again learn to discover
what she desires, who she is, what she wants and is capable of.
She still has a binge now and then (about twice a week): She now
sees it as a signal that she has too high expectations, that she is
going too fast. Louise finally decides to live in a community center
(i.e., a house where rooms are shared by different students) and
applies for a job as a clerk. She switches over to day hospital and
each night goes to the community center. Shortly before her discharge, her last evaluation discussion takes place. Reflecting on her
GAE, she evaluates her progress in the different problem areas as
follows:

A1: I keep drinking a lot of coffee and I wonder if I really want
 to change this, though I can stick better to the fixed times.
A2: I eat less fruit between meals and also feel less swollen.
B1: I again feel more self-confident than a while ago. I can take
 things as they are better, and I panic less (soon). I also have
 the feeling of being myself again in all sorts of situations, and
 so I am also less afraid to utter my own views.
B2: I don't quite understand how all this could change such a lot.
 I can now listen more easily and quietly to other people's problems, try to help them, and then forget about it.
C1: I shall have to keep working on the relationship with my
 father. I have decided to accept his proposal to come more

often. Every 2 weeks may be exaggerated, but it seems regular.

C2: Things are all right outside of the hospital. I feel myself becoming stronger inside, I feel good in my own body, and I have started to appreciate myself better. It is nice to live with other people. I think it is because I have nothing to conceal, which I used to do a lot and in a forced way.

In the course of Louise's treatment, the following strategies and interventions within the group therapy have been significant.

Cognitive Restructuring

Via the diary and later in the group sessions, Louise discloses a whole series of conceptions and thoughts that hamper change in her life:

- I look like a swollen elephant, as though I were pregnant.
- Men are not to be trusted, they only want sex.
- When you show your feelings, people abuse them.
- I should not show that I am uncertain or weak.
- I can't deal with conflicts.
- I should not attach myself to anything or anyone, or else I am lost.

Within the group therapy these conceptions and thoughts are constantly called into question. The other members are often excellent cotherapists; their interventions are often more radical, direct, and effective than those of the therapist. For example, Louise is continually preoccupied with her "pregnant" belly. In the group, Peggy—a bulimic patient who is very overweight—responds violently: "How the hell is it possible that you think you have a big belly? Take a good look at mine. I am still overweight by 40 lb. I can't take your belly complaints anymore, it makes me feel desperate." Louise is very upset about this. The therapist explores this theme with her, and she discovers that the problem is rather her fear of sexuality and pregnancy than just her belly.

Learning Specific Skills

From the assessment of Louise's problems, it clearly appears that she lacks or has not really mastered certain skills such as expressing feelings, starting and discussing conflicts, sharing confidences, uttering one's own views. The group context offers possibilities for practicing these skills. Louise is continually encouraged to utter her feelings. The expression of her own views and her daring to start conflicts are regularly practiced through role playing. Gradually Louise gains more confidence in herself, the group members, and the therapists.

Using Nonspecific Therapy Factors

When, at the completion of the inpatient treatment, we ask Louise what helped her most in the treatment and to which therapeutic factors she attributes her progress, she answers:

> The constant support and encouragement I was given by the group and the team have been extremely important for me. Whatever I did, however I felt, I have always been accepted and given attention. Also, the rules and the structure in the program were extremely important, though I find it hard to admit this. But above all, I was constantly given the message that I could change and that there was hope left for me. This helped me a lot.

It is remarkable how Louise—like most other patients—considers the nonspecific therapeutic factors in particular as extremely important for her progress in the therapy. This is why we try to make maximum use of such factors as offering support, encouragement, and hope.

After her discharge from our center, Louise continued to attend the weekly outpatient group therapy for bulimic patients for about 1 year. In the first months she threatened to relapse into her bulimia, and now and then she felt very depressed. The reason for this was to be found in a few rather unexpected dramatic events in her family of origin: Shortly after her discharge, her mother decompensated again into a depression, and her younger sister was hospitalized for a short time because of a state of total confusion and apathy. Louise was about to hurry home in order to help the other family members. However, she appeared to be strong enough to continue to live her own life and to further extend her positive evolution. "I had to fight awfully hard for my own life, often all by myself, so I think they will have to make it by themselves as well now," Louise writes in her diary. In the follow-up, 2 years after her discharge from our center, Louise appears to do very well. Binge eating and vomiting occur only sporadically (at most once a month). She studies, lives with a friend, and feels satisfied with her life.

6

Hypnotherapy

Encouraged by enthusiastic case studies and the finding that BN patients are easily hypnotizable subjects, we have also incorporated hypnotic techniques in our treatment (see Vanderlinden & Vandereycken, 1988c, 1990). In the following part we shall describe when and how hypnotherapeutic techniques can be integrated into a multidimensional approach.

GENERAL CHARACTERISTICS

Hypnotic experience is a natural phenomenon in everyday life. For example, we may be so emotionally involved in watching a film or reading a book that we barely realize that the phone is ringing. Or while driving home, we may be so deeply absorbed in thoughts that we pass the right exit. In these situations we assume that the subject is in a state of spontaneous—though light—hypnotic trance. A hypnotic state can be described as an altered state of consciousness, with an increased concentration on a limited perception. During hypnosis individuals are deeply absorbed by an internal experience and their imagery is greatly increased.

As to its clinical applications, we don't consider hypnosis as a treatment method on its own. In our opinion, hypnotherapeutic techniques should always be combined with and integrated into an existing therapeutic framework. We believe that the incorporation of hypnosis in a multidimensional treatment may facilitate the course and outcome of therapy. Whenever the use of hypnotic techniques seem indicated, we apply them in individual sessions and according to the different phases in the therapy process. In the beginning, the therapist will introduce hypnotic techniques for symptom reduction. Only after patients have regained some control over their eating behavior will hypnoanalytic and exploring techniques be employed. Ego-strengthening techniques are used throughout the whole treatment.

SPECIFIC HYPNOTHERAPEUTIC STRATEGIES

Teaching Self-Hypnosis as a Relaxation Technique

Clinical experience and findings from our ongoing research on dissociation in eating disorders (see Chapter 2) have taught us that most BN patients are easily hypnotizable subjects. The best test to assess this hypnotizability is to provide a hypnosis induction. Obviously, misconceptions and prejudices concerning hypnosis should be corrected beforehand. Patients are told that hypnosis is a technique that can easily be learned by anyone and that the hypnotic state can help them within a short time to feel more relaxed and to keep calm in future moments of crisis.

We usually offer patients a formal hypnosis induction: We start with an eye-fixation technique (choosing a focus), continue with a few deepening techniques (breathing, descending an escalator, arm levitation, etc.), and conclude with a short future-oriented fantasy. In the latter, patients attempt to imagine finding themselves in a place where they can feel peaceful, safe, and protected; recover a while; and thus gradually enable themselves to relax. In patients who tend to resist this direct approach, we may switch over to a nondirective (Ericksonian) induction, although this seldom occurs. BN patients generally prefer a distinctly structured hypnosis induction. The basic exercise is recorded on an audiocassette, and patients are asked to practice with it every day at home (if possible, before and after meals). In this way patients are trained in self-hypnosis as a relaxation technique. Each time after completion of the exercise, they are asked to judge the depth of relaxation on a 10-point scale (0 = absence of relaxation, 10 = deepest relaxation) and to note this in their diary. This gives the therapist a subjective estimation of possible progression and/or difficulties in the self-hypnosis.

Teaching Self-Control Techniques

Hypnotic techniques will be incorporated in the initial treatment phase for teaching step-by-step self-control over the eating pattern. Above all, it is essential to agree with patients on a realistic goal regarding eating pattern and weight. The aim is to stabilize the weight and to gradually reduce the binges. Vomiting and purging should be stopped as soon as possible. A cognitive-behavioral approach promoting self-control over the eating behavior (see Chapter 4) may often be combined with hypnotic techniques. During the basic hypnosis exercise it might be suggested that the patients will each day choose a moment to accurately fill in the diary and that completing the diary daily will bring them comfort and release.

. . . And each time again you look forward to the moment you retire to review quietly your day and to fill in your diary. You may be amazed at your own concentration in these moments and at your feeling of being satisfied afterward and at your being able to peacefully prepare yourself for a deep, relaxing sleep . . .

A basic goal in the beginning of therapy is the *normalization of the eating behavior*. Hypnosis can be introduced to teach patients to resume a regular and normal eating pattern (to stop the bingeing-vomiting-purging cycle) and to become again more conscious of feelings of hunger and satiation. For example, the patient may be asked to imagine having a normal breakfast in the morning.

Imagine yourself getting up in the morning. You may first take a shower or do some gymnastics to be wide awake and to learn even more consciously to eat normally again . . . The breakfast table is laid. You sit down at the table and decide for yourself what you would like to eat. You may feel your stomach's signaling that you are hungry. Your stomach feels empty. . . And at each bite you concentrate on the food in your mouth, on its taste. You chew quietly . . . Your stomach will gradually indicate when you have had enough. You may even discover certain signals of your having eaten enough . . . And then you can terminate the meal with a feeling of satisfaction. Afterward you relax a little, quietly dreaming off and enjoying the memory of a pleasant vacation . . .

A realistic objective at the beginning of the treatment is to reduce the binges gradually instead of stopping them immediately. Patients may be asked to plan one or more binges a week at a fixed time, with food they do not like. The vomiting, however, should be stopped as soon as possible or at least postponed as long as possible.

Julia is given the task to plan a binge three times a week (instead of three times a day): on Monday, Wednesday, and Friday at 7 P.M., exclusively with canned peas and carrots. In order to prevent her from vomiting after each binge, Julia has to leave the house at once and pay a visit to the woman next door for at least half an hour.

Patients may also be invited to first experience during hypnosis how they can plan to binge and stop vomiting. The responses to this suggestion vary markedly. A small group refuses adamantly: Often this is a signal of insufficient motivation or weak therapeutic alliance. Nevertheless, most patients comply with this proposal and have the positive experience of being able to imagine something that they before labeled as impossible (planned bingeing and not vomiting). In other patients, this procedure has a paradoxical effect: They find it loathsome to have to binge and then feel disgusted about carrying out this task. An important advantage of the task of bingeing during hypnosis is that it may provide the therapist with a lot of information on what the patient really feels and thinks before, during, and after bingeing.

> Sylvia hesitatingly agrees to the suggestion to imagine a binge during hypnosis. During the exercise we notice that she becomes anxious. She feels a tension throughout her body, and bingeing is the only thought that occupies her mind. She feels an intense sadness and starts crying. The binge happens as quick as lightning; it is "only half-conscious," Sylvia tells us. After that, she feels herself guilty, bad, loathsome, and swollen and wants to go vomit. The therapist then asks her to imagine postponing the vomiting a while by reading a fascinating book, which she hardly manages to do.

Enhancing Motivation for Change

Besides self-monitoring (diary) and stimulus control techniques, we often introduce other strategies to enhance self-control over the eating behavior and motivation for change: the strategy of positive and negative consequences. Patients are asked to imagine a bulimia-free life in the future and to write down all its positive consequences. They are also asked to specify all negative consequences if they go on with bingeing and vomiting. Next, the therapist uses this information during hypnosis to enhance patients' motivation for change.

> During hypnosis Ellen is asked to make a short trip into the future for a while, and next the therapist introduces and exaggerates all the negative consequences of her overeating and vomiting: "Whenever the urge to binge is present, your subconscious mind will help you remember all the negative consequences and dangers of bingeing and vomiting. You are ruining your body, especially

your teeth, and you are losing your hair. You are destroying your self-esteem and vitality, and you become more and more isolated. You get into serious financial trouble . . ."

It may also be suggested that the patient begins to feel even worse and sicker after vomiting than before. However, in another exercise the positive consequences of stopping binges may be overaccentuated.

"If you gradually stop bingeing and learn to eat regularly and normally again, you will become more and more aware of all the positive consequences for you. You gradually regain your self-confidence and self-esteem. You feel more energy and vitality. You develop new interests. You make new contacts with peers, and you feel good in a healthier body . . ."

Exploring Ambivalence Toward Change

We have already mentioned the ambivalence that is nearly always present in BN patients with regard to therapeutic progress. The previous task, writing down all positive and negative consequences of normalizing the eating behavior, often makes patients realize that a bulimia-free future may also induce anxiety: for instance, about becoming more independent and living on one's own or exploring conflicts in the marital relationship. Instead of openly discussing the patient's ambivalent attitudes with regard to changes, the therapist can easily explore these in an indirect way by means of hypnotherapeutic techniques such as ideomotor questioning and finger signaling with the seven questions of Le Cron (Cheek & Le Cron, 1968; Wright & Wright, 1982). In this technique, patients are told that their "unconscious mind" will reveal information about their problem that was up to now inaccessible. The unconscious mind can then answer questions by "involuntary" finger responses indicating yes or no (*ideomotor signaling*). After having defined finger signals for yes and no, patients can be asked to signal whether there is something—an unconscious part of their personality—that inhibits them in the changing process. Subsequently, the ambivalent attitude can be further analyzed with the seven questions of *Le Cron*, which can be answered by finger signals:

1. Does the symptom serve a purpose; is something pleasant achieved or something annoying avoided by it?
2. Is it the result of an inner conflict, of something you would like to but cannot or may not do?
3. Is the problem caused by a feeling of guilt and the idea of deserving to be punished for it?
4. Is it a result of identification with someone else?
5. Is the problem caused by a trauma, a nasty event in the past?
6. Is it a result of your imagination, of a remark made about you while you were in a responsive emotional state?
7. Is the problem a result of body language, as if you wanted to express something psychological on a physical level, such as headache when somebody "is bugging you" and stomachache and vomiting because something "is lying heavy on your stomach"?

Esther, a 31-year-old single woman with a severe BN for more than 16 years, responds enthusiastically to the suggested self-control procedures (diary, stimulus control), and she practices her self-hypnosis several times a day. As soon as the bulimia decreases a little, as she regains more control of her eating pattern, Esther becomes tense, anxious, and depressed, and she no longer follows the agreements that had been made. She feels that "something inside doesn't want to cooperate anymore."

We then propose to her that we explore the ambivalent attitude by means of the ideomotor questioning (with finger signaling and the seven questions of Le Cron). Exploration of her ambivalent state reveals that the bulimic symptoms are protecting Esther against the

fear of growing up. She feels guilty whenever she distances herself
from her mother, with whom she has a very strong tie. The encouragement to live on her own results in increased feelings of guilt,
which in turn increases the binges again. Through vomiting, she
also appears to express her anger and rage toward her mother,
who—according to Esther—is overprotecting her and cannot let
go of her.

These hypnotherapeutic strategies may help both therapist and
patient in the exploration and understanding of areas of ambivalence. It can also heighten patients' awareness and understanding
of the psychological meaning of their ambivalent state.

Exploring the Dissociated State

The existence of a dissociated state in BN patients has been discussed before (see Chapter 2). These patients regularly mention that
they have the feeling of changing into a different personality during
their binges.

- "It is as if it isn't me while I am bingeing."
- "It is as if something has taken me over."
- "I believe that some unknown part inside me refuses to stop
  bingeing."
- "I am continually engaged in a fight against myself."
- "In my head there is something switching off and on, and
  then there is only one desire: to binge, and nothing but binge.
  Only after vomiting do I have the feeling to awaken and to
  become myself again."

Such descriptions made us infer the presence of an ego-dissociated
state in these patients. The concept of dissociation means that a
particular thought or whole complex of thoughts with the accompanying feelings escapes the control and sometimes the knowledge
of the personal consciousness. By dissociated ego state is meant the

escape of a particular ego state from the conscious mind. According to Watkins and Watkins (1982), an ego state is an organized complex of behaviors, thoughts, and experiences whose elements are bound together by some common principle, but separated from another ego state by boundaries that are more or less permeable. Each ego state constitutes a kind of "subself," which has more or less individual autonomy in relation to other states and to the entire personality. Ego states may be created and dissociated or split off from the conscious mind when the patient is confronted by a traumatic experience (Vanderlinden et al., 1990). When such an ego state is split off or dissociated from the conscious mind, the boundaries between the different ego states are no longer permeable and become rigid. These ego states can be activated again under hypnosis (Torem, 1987; Vanderlinden & Vandereycken, 1990) and thus be further explored.

The ego state therapy in BN patients runs in several phases:

1. When the therapist presumes—for instance, on the basis of the description of the binge by the patient—that a dissociated ego state is present, he or she will first ask the permission of the patient's unconscious mind to explore the hidden ego state that provokes the bulimia.
2. Next the patient is asked to imagine having a binge and to concentrate on the "bulimic part" inside. It is explained that this might help the patient to come in touch with the unknown bulimic part. The therapist can then ask the bulimic part to make itself known.
3. As soon as that part has made itself known, the therapist thanks it for its appearance and asks: "What is your name?"
4. After that, the therapist will try to find out how old the patient was when that part first manifested itself and what its intention was. We often observe that the bulimic

part pursued a specific goal: for instance, to protect or to comfort the patient, or to punish the patient for feelings of guilt.

5. At this stage, the therapist reformulates in a positive way the purpose of the bulimic part but asks that part if it wants to cooperate to find new, more effective ways to achieve this goal (such as comforting or protecting in a different way). A negotiation process then arises between the patient and the bulimic part to agree on a more constructive and effective approach (e.g., to comfort the patient).

6. The bulimic part is then asked to try out this new method during the following week and is thanked for its cooperation. It is important that the patient learn that the bulimia should not be considered an enemy that will have to be conquered time and again, but that the bulimic part may become an ally signaling that the patient must reflect upon his or her life and plan some concrete change.

Judith, a 23-year-old BN patient, describes in her diary how she can hardly remember what she did during one of her binges, or what she had binged. "Afterwards, it is like I am waking up out of a nightmare or as if I am switching into another personality."

Therapist: While you are enjoying your trance state, you can come in touch with that "part" in you that makes you feel anxious and forces you to binge and vomit. And that part can present itself and make itself known to you and communicate with us as through Judith's voice.

Judith: (after a long pause) Mother . . .

Therapist: When did "mother" come in Judith's life?

Judith: When she was 14.

Therapist: Why did "mother" appear in Judith's life?

Judith: I wanted to protect Judith against the dangers of the outside world. She was very afraid to grow up and to become more independent.

Therapist: So, "mother" appeared to protect and support Judith whenever she felt anxious . . .

A negotiation then arises between "mother," Judith, and the therapist: The therapist latter suggests that "mother" may help Judith by inducing her to make new social contacts during the next week.

Exploring and Coping With Traumatic Events

In many cases, the patient's bulimia conceals traumatic events and/or unsolved conflicts of a highly emotional nature (see Chapter 2). These traumatic events might be incest, rape, physical abuse, extreme lack of affection, or involvement in chronic marital discord. In an ongoing study at our hospital, we found that 36% in a group of 50 eating disorder patients had been victimized by traumatic experiences (Vanderlinden et al., 1990). When comparing several subgroups we found the highest scores for trauma in the bulimic (46%) and the atypical eating disorder groups (66%). Remarkably enough, we noticed that the scores on both hypnotizability and dissociation were related to the presence of traumatic experiences. Dissociation seems to be a kind of survival mechanism in these patients to cope with painful, traumatic experiences. These events are often repressed or dissociated from the conscious mind. Hypnosis can be useful in the detection of such traumatic experiences. Besides the previously described technique of ideomotor questioning by means of the seven questions of Le Cron, we regularly make use of the "*affect bridge technique*" of Watkins (1971). In this exploration technique the often strong and vivid emotions (such as anxiety, agitation, depression) are used as a bridge to the past, to one or more specific situations that the patient will remember and that will make the feelings understandable.

Sandy, a 29-year-old, single BN patient, suddenly feels a severe pain welling up in her whenever she concentrates on the feelings that usually precede her binges. Suddenly she sees a dark space: She is 4 years old and left behind all alone at home by her parents, who went out dancing. Next she describes several similar situations where she felt rejected and abandoned by her parents as she hears her parents quarreling and her mother calling for help. In the therapy Sandy then discovers how the binges helped her to feel more peaceful and to distance herself from the escalating fights between her parents and from the feeling of being unloved. She writes in her diary: "If I do not binge, the pain and sadness become so strong that I am sometimes afraid that I will go mad and might destroy myself completely." At first the eating made her feel loved, but later bingeing and purging were used as a symbolic expression of hate and anger.

The affect bridge technique often uncovers painful experiences and pictures of the past of a highly emotional nature. During these moments the therapist should provide the patient as much support and understanding as possible. Next, the therapist may decide to start with the working through of these experiences.

After the hypnosis induction with the affect bridge technique, Mary suddenly starts trembling and shaking violently. She feels anxious and bursts into tears. She then sees herself as a 6-year-old child lying in a dark room in a hospital. Because of an accident she had to stay in bed in the dark for 25 days. During her stay in the hospital, Mary had felt awful, lonely, and anxious. Only when the meals were brought had there been some contact, and while eating she felt a bit more peaceful. This is how she learned that eating, and later on bingeing, helped her to deal with situations of anxiety. Through an age-regression technique, the present adult was asked to comfort the child she had been, to reassure her, and make it clear to her that she didn't need to be frightened in the dark room.

Other techniques that can be applied in dealing with a traumatic event are implosive desensitization and silent abreaction (Edelstein,

1982). *Implosive desensitization* is a sort of friendly and progressive flooding technique in which the patient reexperiences time and again the feelings about the traumatic event, with interruptions, until the feelings have sufficiently decreased in strength. The therapist then applies the affect bridge technique again to make the patient reexperience these feelings until a next pause is reached in the story. The confrontation is repeated until the tension gradually decreases to a level that is tolerable for the patient.

Ann, a 30-year-old successful business woman, has been secretly bingeing and vomiting for more than 14 years. When she calls us, this is the very first time she has sought help. Through the affect bridge technique, she sees herself as a 7-year-old girl accidentally walking into her mother's bedroom and witnessing her mother with a strange man. She runs away yelling, feels suddenly sick, and throws up all her food. Since the age of about 16, and specifically since the first sexual approach by boys, Ann has often felt suddenly anxious and sick. She then vomits for reasons totally unknown to her. She also gradually starts bingeing.

During hypnosis she is repeatedly asked to reexperience this former situation until the feelings of anxiety become tolerable. But now an enormous anger rises in her: Ann remembers how her mother threatened her the morning after the adultery and ordered her never to talk about it to anyone. This made her intensely furious. This repressed anger can now be uttered through the *silent abreaction*. Ann is asked to imagine herself in a safe place watching television pictures in which she sees how she abreacts her long years of repressed fury toward her mother. It is also made clear to her that she need not feel guilty about this.

Another technique to work through traumatic experiences more indirectly is to invite the patient to abreact—for instance, her feelings of aggression—in a symbolic or metaphoric manner. The patient is then asked under trance to fantasize—for example, that she walks, together with someone she feels very safe with, in a wood during springtime. She is invited to search for a kind of bat or another object to beat with. Next she is told that a special tree, symbolizing everything that made her so angry and sad in life, is situated somewhere in this wood. Once she discovers this tree, the patient is invited to beat on it with her bat as heavily as she wants. Meanwhile suggestions are given of getting rid of her aggressive feelings and hence becoming less tense, more relaxed. We recommend this technique in the case of long-lasting sexual abuse, since a direct confrontation with the offender under hypnosis is often impossible or provokes too much anxiety.

In between, the patients are given the task to practice self-hypnosis daily in order to learn to relax more and better. Gradually, many patients detect that they no longer need to escape or repress the feelings that precede the binges (such as anxiety, emptiness, depression), but that these feelings can help them to discover the psychological meaning of their bulimia. The urge to binge is then redefined as an indirect need for change or as a clear sign of the urgent need for questioning their feelings and restructuring their lives.

Correcting Unrealistic Conceptions

BN patients continually put negative labels on themselves: They describe and perceive themselves as incompetent, weak, inferior, ugly, stupid, ridiculous, childish, infantile, immature, dependent. . . . These negative labels are often suggested to the patient by other family members as indirect "hypnoticlike" messages (see Chapter 7). The unrealistic and negative thoughts concern mainly eating habits, weight, body shape, relationships, sexuality, perfectionistic attitudes. These negative ideas help to maintain the "bulimic identity" and make change and growth extremely difficult. On the basis of the patient's diary, the therapist can detect these irrational and inadequate self-perceptions. Hypnosis can then be combined with cognitive restructuring techniques in order to question and change the bulimic identity.

> Marcia, a 23-year-old BN patient also presenting with severe agoraphobia, describes herself as follows: "I shall never make anything of my life, I am stupid because I haven't got a single certificate, and my body size is like an elephant. No one will ever want to have a relationship with me; besides I am much too childish and infantile for that." Marcia is given the task to note in her diary each day three positive experiences or ideas about herself. These positive labels are then used in a hypnotic exercise in which Marcia imagines herself in the near future: she will become more and more aware of her strengths and learn to better accept her weaknesses. She is then given the task to plan a trip, and Marcia books a group travel to Greece. Before, she is asked during a hypnosis session to picture herself in Greece for a while and to imagine different group members showing interest in her person. She also imagines herself enjoying these contacts and being flattered now and then by certain attentions. A few weeks later we see Marcia back and she appears to have experienced for the first time what it means to have "butterflies in one's stomach." She is in love with a young man who in turn shows much interest in her!

Promoting and Stimulating Independence

Since our follow-up data showed a better outcome for patients (older than 18 years) who leave the family home to live on their own, in a foster family, or a community center (Vanderlinden & Vandereycken, 1987), we nearly systematically encourage our older patients to make this important step. Also in married patients or those who have been living on their own for some time, the emotional distancing from the family of origin appears to have a crucial significance for a favorable course of therapy (see Chapter 7). Hypnosis can be used to prepare patients for this crucial life transition. The therapist can ask patients to project themselves into the future during trance and to imagine how they gradually become emotionally more independent from their parents and feel stronger and better balanced to plan their own life by themselves. In between, the therapist provides ego-strengthening suggestions. Many patients express their dependence on their family in metaphorical descriptions. For instance: "I have the feeling of being still tied to my home by my umbilical cord" and "I am always longing for that 'warm nest' at home." These metaphorical descriptions can be used during hypnosis to promote patient growth and autonomy. Indirect suggestions, metaphors, and anecdotes are especially indicated for those patients with a strong fear of change and independence.

> Rita, 24 years of age, has been suffering from severe BN for more than 8 years. She is still extremely dependent upon her parents, although she was living on her own during the week for quite some time. On the weekend she always seeks refuge in her family home, "in the family nest." During the trance, Rita is asked to picture this family nest and to look over the horizon from there, observing attractive spots in the surroundings. Now and then she is instructed to fly out of the nest in order to explore the environment. Gradually, the experiences outside of the nest begin to fascinate her more and more, and she then decides to construct a nest for herself elsewhere . . .

Final Considerations

From our—still limited—experience we believe that the incorporation of hypnotic techniques in a multidimensional treatment has several advantages:

• Most bulimic patients are easily hypnotizable subjects.

- Hypnotic techniques can easily be combined with cognitive behavioral strategies (namely, self-control procedures).
- The function of the bulimia can be explored more quickly and thoroughly by means of hypnosis.
- Hypnosis may help patients to reintegrate the dissociated "bulimic part" of themselves into their personal life.
- Hypnosis will be of special help in the uncovering and working through (abreaction) of traumatic experiences.

In conclusion, hypnotic techniques can facilitate the therapeutic process to a great extent. However, in addition to these enthusiastic reports, a few critical considerations and warnings are certainly indicated. Hypnosis is neither a magical trick nor a new treatment, but a method that should be integrated within an existing therapeutic frame of reference. Moreover, there is urgent need of more detailed research, for example, on the nature or extent of the dissociated state in BN patients and its possible relation with the therapeutic result.

CASE EXAMPLE

This is the story of the therapy of Dina, a 24-year-old single woman who was referred to us for treatment of a long-lasting (more than 6 years) BN accompanied by depression and daily abuse of appetite suppressants. The treatment was carried out on an outpatient basis and consisted of 40 sessions spread over 2 years. The use of hypnotic techniques was a crucial element in this treatment.

Some Background Data

Dina lives on her own and studies archeology. The bulimia, purging, and abuse of appetite suppressants started at the age of about

18, when she decided to live on her own. Dina has few good memories of her childhood and early youth. Her father has been disabled
for years because of "nervous problems." He is regularly verbally
aggressive and afterward does not speak a word for weeks. Whenever
her parents quarrel, Dina always tries to support her mother. Even
now that she lives on her own, her mother regularly calls in for
help. Dina is the third of four daughters; two of her sisters also
appear to have eating disorders and are overweight. In spite of the
long duration of the bulimia, Dina has never talked to anyone in
her family about her binges. Only the family doctor, whom she
consulted recently, knows about the binges and referred Dina to
our center for treatment. Throughout the treatment Dina refused
adamantly to involve either her parents or sisters. Considering her
strong motivation for change, we decided to start with individual
therapy. Hereafter follows a survey of the principal hypnotherapeutic
techniques that were successively applied in the outpatient
treatment.

Relaxation Through Self-Hypnosis

Dina, who has had some experience with yoga, reacts enthusiastically when we propose relaxation with the self-hypnosis practice. Especially in the evening she feels anxious and tense and
wonders if she could indeed relax better through self-hypnosis.
As a first exercise, we suggest an arm levitation technique. Dina
appears to possess very good hypnotic skills. We also introduce
an exercise in which she is asked to remember a particular vacation in which she felt very fine and happy. This succeeds fairly
enough and we then suggest, to "anchor" these positive feelings,
pressing the left middle finger and the left thumb on each other
(a cue for relaxation conditioning). This will be her secret
weapon for learning to feel herself more peaceful in frightening
situations.

Teaching Self-Control Techniques

At the beginning of the treatment, Dina has an enormous binge almost every night. These binges drastically increased her weight from 104 to 160 lb. She feels miserable, fat, and ugly, and continually tries to hide her body. We then make the usual agreements to have three meals per day at fixed times. She will keep a diary and try to identify possible risk situations for bulimia. The first objective is the stabilization of her weight. In order to help Dina to gain more control of her eating pattern and to enhance her motivation, we first make use of the *strategy of positive and negative consequences*. During a guided-imagery exercise (3 months ahead in the future) the following suggestions are made: "You may notice already how your weight has decreased. You stick to your three daily meals and you feel healthier. You feel more relaxed, satisfied, and you begin to perceive your future positive again. You look forward again to meeting other people . . ." After that, Dina is asked to imagine how she will feel if she goes on bingeing: ". . . and then you may see how much more weight you have put on, you look totally swollen. Your self-esteem is very low, you are becoming more anxious . . . You feel constantly tired, very heavy, and you hide yourself from others . . ."

After a few months, Dina has managed to normalize her eating pattern somewhat and her weight begins to decrease slowly, although the bulimia still emerges at least once a week. Contrary to the time before the treatment, she now begins to realize that the bingeing occurs exclusively in specific situations, mostly during or immediately after the weekends when she stays at her parents'. Next we decide to further explore the underlying dynamics and meaning of the bulimia. This will be the principal part in Dina's further treatment.

Exploration of Underlying Significance and Dynamics

During a first exploration of the underlying meaning and/or function of the bulimia, we make use of the seven questions of Le Cron.
Two questions are answered positively: "Is the bulimia a result of
an inner conflict, of something you would like to do, but cannot
or may not do? Is the bulimia caused by a trauma, a nasty event
in the past?" Dina's subconscious is asked to help her to go back
to the time when the nasty event(s) occurred. Dina suddenly sees
herself as a 5-year-old child sitting beneath the stairs, huddled up
in anxiety. She can hear her mother, who is seriously ill, begging
her father to call for the doctor, but father refuses. Mother calls
out louder and louder: "Call for the doctor, for I am dying." Dina
starts trembling and crying, she is afraid that mother will die. She
can also hear the other children cry. Father then also starts bellowing
against the other children and shouts out to them "to shut their
traps." All the children are sent upstairs without supper. At night,
Dina cannot sleep; she is anxious and hungry, and goes into the
kitchen. After eating she feels a little more peaceful and manages
to get some sleep. This situation will be brought back several times
during hypnosis later on in the treatment.

After this hypnotic exercise, Dina realizes that both the binges
and the anxiety at home try to make it clear to her that she still
finds it hard to deal with particular nasty events from the past,
which even now still occur regularly (such as violent escalating
fights between her parents). She also realizes that she has always
tried to solve her parents' quarrels and how she anxiously attempts
to avoid conflicts and quarrels in her relationships outside of the
family. Dina is known to be the exemplary daughter, always ready
to help ("You can ask her anything, she will never refuse to help").

Coping With Traumatic Experiences

During the following weeks Dina experiences intense feelings of hatred against her father. These become so strong that she decides, for the time being, to stop seeing her parents on the weekends. During the next hypnotic exercise, there is an attempt to deal somehow with these strong feelings of hatred against her father. After hypnosis induction, Dina is asked to think about her father and to let all her feelings come up normally. She feels enormous anger, but at the same time also anxiety and sadness. She is encouraged to "throw out" these feelings. She sees all kinds of dark, black stones, which she throws away one by one until she feels somewhat relieved. After that, she puts all the stones in a large bag, which is dumped deep into the sea from a boat. She sees the bag sinking to the bottom of the sea as quick as lightning . . .

Together with this exercise, some thought is also given to her father's family of origin, in the hope that Dina may learn to understand why her father is regularly so hard and aggressive. She then tells us how father himself grew up in a family that was traumatized when his own father (Dina's grandfather) was killed in a bombardment in World War II. Her father, who was a boy of 15 and the eldest son of a family with 10 children, had to replace his deceased father. In the therapy Dina further discovers how her father had in fact never accepted the responsibility of this fatherhood (parentification), which had been brusquely forced upon him at the age of 15. Perhaps this explains his problems with the father role in the family that he later created himself. These thoughts help Dina to deal in a more adequate way with her feelings toward her father.

Promoting and Stimulating Independence

Dina gradually becomes more and more conscious of the fact that she is always depending on other people. She avoids conflicts, never utters her own views, and always nods yes. She now clearly sees the connection with the experiences in her family of origin, but still feels uncertain and hardly dares to express her own views. Different hypnotic sessions are now planned in which learning to express one's views, daring to have a difference of opinion, and gradually gaining more self-confidence are dealt with. Concrete situations such as daring to say no to a girlfriend asking her to help her clean up and calling up her parents to tell them she is not coming to see them on the weekend are first practiced under hypnosis.

In order to enhance her independence from her family of origin, we also make use of a hypnotic exercise, in which Dina imagines herself starting on an exploratory travel into the wide world—as a sort of metaphor promoting her separation-individuation process. Traveling was also a dream Dina had been cherishing for years. During the exercise it is suggested how she can, by traveling alone, learn to widen her horizon, to make new contacts, and, above all, to develop a strong feeling of self-confidence and belief in her own capacities and abilities. A few months later, Dina interrupts the therapy for about 2 months and travels to Southeast Asia, a unique and extremely instructive experience.

Other exercises are focused rather on general ego strengthening, in which we make use, among other things, of the *tree fantasy exercise for ego strength* of Krystal (1982). During this exercise Dina imagines that she can, like a tree, via the roots of mother (earth) and the branches of father, receive the things her actual parents could not always give. Finally, during her examination periods at the university, we offer her a hypnotic exercise for good concentration, quiet studying, and relaxed feelings during exams. Dina obtains excellent results.

Epilogue

Dina's evolution is favorable. Her eating pattern is completely normal, and she manages to stabilize her weight around 110 lb. She has lost about 50 lb, without any special diets, just by eating and exercising regularly. She mostly manages to keep sufficient distance from her parents, although sometimes she still feels herself influenced by their remarks and criticism. After 1½ years of therapy, we propose to stop the treatment. Still, a few final sessions are planned. Shortly after this, Dina calls unexpectedly, telling us that she has been swallowing appetite suppressants again for a few days. She is panicky about this, for she does not know why she did it. In the next session it appears that she is afraid to stop therapy. She has been feeling lonely again recently, and the appetite suppressants are a kind of alarm signal "that she still might use some more support." We take her message seriously and decide to continue the treatment for some more months (one single session per month). Dina further evolves favorably. At the follow-up, 1 year after completion of the therapy, everything goes well and she feels rather satisfied with her life.

7

Family Therapy

In contrast to the flood of publications about the family therapeutic approach to anorexia nervosa, surprisingly little attention has been paid in the literature to the application of family therapy in BN. Most therapists still appear to regard the BN patient as a separate individual and pay little or no attention to the family system or the broader psychosocial context. In the literature we found only a few—though enthusiastic—case studies on the use of family therapy in BN. Some authors have described a systematic family approach to BN (Schwartz et al., 1985; Root et al., 1986; Vandereycken et al., 1989; Vanderlinden & Vandereycken, 1989). Except for the study done by Russell and coworkers (1987, see Chapter 2), controlled research on the effectiveness of family therapy in BN is almost completely lacking.

How can we explain that the family of the BN patient has been ignored by therapists for such a long time? The most obvious explanation may be that this peculiar eating disorder has only recently (since the early 1980s) caught the attention of therapists. Furthermore, the neglect of the family may also be attributed to the fact that bulimics tend to conceal their problematic behavior— though often because of strong feelings of shame and/or guilt—from their families and the outside world. Finally, the absence of consideration of the family context in the literature on bulimia can also be ascribed to the average age (20 to 25 years) of BN patients, which is higher than that of anorexia patients. Many of them have been living on their own for some time and seem not to take part anymore in their family of origin. In this chapter we shall illustrate our own experiences with more than 150 bulimic families. We shall describe the principal family therapeutic strategies, interventions, and possible pitfalls.

GENERAL CHARACTERISTICS

It is essential, in our opinion, that the family therapist have a central and coordinating function in the inpatient or outpatient treatment team (Vandereycken et al., 1989). In our hospital, for instance, the family therapist coordinates different functions: doing the intake interview and, subsequently, being actively involved as a therapist in both family and group therapy. In between, the family therapist can also—in the case of a severe crisis—invite the bulimic patient to an individual interview, or the patient can request an individual session.

The family therapeutic approach can best be described as a form of directive family therapy (Lange & van der Hart, 1983): a pragmatic, eclectic, and flexible approach, wherein elements of structural, strategic, and behavioral family therapy are combined. The main focus is on the here-and-now situation: There is an attempt to bring about change in the actual problems, such as they are presented by the family. In that sense, the bulimic symptomatology is nearly always used as a first entrance into the family system. Often interviews are planned with the separate subsystems: parents separately and the patient together with siblings. Not infrequently the families of origin of both parents are also involved in the treatment for a short time. The decision for this is based on a thorough functional analysis of the BN within the family system. The main question is whether the bulimia plays a role or has a special function within the family system and/or how the eating disorder is possibly interwoven with a dysfunctional family context. Experience has taught us that treatment itself is the best way to test, reformulate, and adjust our clinical hypotheses.

As mentioned repeatedly, the therapeutic process passes through different phases or stages, each of them necessitating specific clinical strategies and interventions. The following description of these phases is offered only as a flexible framework since the therapeutic process obviously can take different turnings according to each family's dynamics.

BEGINNING PHASE: ASSESSING AND PREPARING FOR CHANGE

It is a general rule in our treatment to invite the family and/or partner to the first interview. Not infrequently, patients first refuse to invite their parents because they prefer to keep the bulimia secret.

> Angelica, a 26-year-old, single BN patient, has had daily binges followed by self-induced vomiting for some 3 years. The bulimia started when she left home to live on her own 3 years ago, after terrible fights with her parents about her leaving. Angelica explicitly requests us not to invite her parents, who know nothing about her problems. She does not want to lose face: Discussing her problems with her parents would be admitting her "failure."

In such a situation, the patient will first be invited individually. During this interview, however, there will be an attempt to gain permission to invite the parents. We have indeed repeatedly observed in our practice how strong the ties of loyalty with the family of origin still are, in spite of the often many years that the BN patient has existed seemingly independently. During the first interview, the family therapist will invite all family members to express their own views and will try to construct a positive *working alliance* with all of them. The therapist needs to realize that it might be the first time for these family members to start talking together overtly and directly about the bulimia and other problems.

A tense and anxious atmosphere often reigns in the therapy room during the first interview: We encourage the family to put these feelings (anxiety, shame, disappointment, powerlessness, grief, anger, aggression) into words. We explicitly mention that the question of who is to blame or guilty is irrelevant and senseless. What matters is whether the patient, with the support of the family (partner), is ready to deal with these problems in the here and now. We are often struck by the extreme denial of the parents and/or other family members: For months or sometimes many years, they had never "noticed" anything of the bingeing or vomiting in their child (sibling or spouse)! Not infrequently family members appear to be astonishingly blind to the constant disappearance of food supplies or never notice the sour smell of vomitus in the toilet. And even when they do suspect something, they often avoid talking about it openly.

> Mary, a 28-year-old schoolmistress, has had daily binges followed by vomiting for 7 years. At home, there had never been any talk of the vomitus in the toilet and the constant disappearance of food from the kitchen cupboard, until her admission to the hospital. Her mother, who had been on bad terms with her husband for years, had thought all the time that it was he who had been vomiting on account of a "liver disorder"!

The gravity of the bulimic symptomatology is often strongly denied by both patient and other family members. Informing the family about the seriousness and dangers of bingeing and vomiting (causing psychobiological deterioration, e.g., electrolyte disturbances) should therefore be rated among the principal tasks of the therapist. For this purpose, our BN patients are given a special information brochure about the risks of bingeing, vomiting, and purging (Appendix C). Moreover, this brochure also contains advice and a few practical guidelines for regaining control over the eating pattern step by step.

Central to this initial phase is, obviously, a functional analysis of the bulimia against the background of the family system (see Figure 4). First, the therapist should focus on the family system and collect the following information: family structure and mutual coalitions, phase in the family life cycle, transgenerational influences, and family functioning on different levels (how does the family behave, think, and feel with regard to the problem?). Most BN families with whom we work in our treatment center can be described as chaotic and unstructured: Boundaries, rules, and agreements are lacking; tensions and conflicts are not directly or overtly discussed and thus remain unsolved. These family histories often include substance abuse and/or mood disorders in the parents and victimization (physical violence and/or sexual abuse) of the patient. In spite of (c)overt tensions and conflicts, the family members are often tied to one another by strong bonds of loyalty. The BN patient may have tried, for instance, to leave home and settle down else-

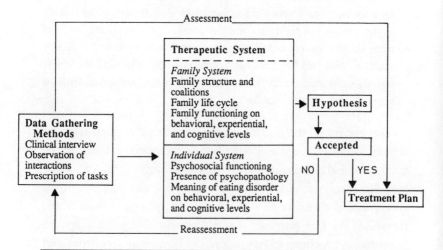

Figure 4. Different Steps in the Functional Analysis.

where independently, but failed to do so. The bulimia seems then to be a cry for help, an attempt to separate and differentiate oneself from the chaos of the family.

> Marlene, 25 years of age, is the eldest daughter in a family with three children. When she was 12, severe conflicts arose between her parents, and her mother started drinking. Marlene was assigned the function of head of the family in her early youth (her father was always out of the house), and she also started drinking and bingeing secretly. Her mother continually sought support in Marlene, and both parents made her arbitrator in their quarrels. At the age of 16, Marlene fled from home and got lost in the drug world. But she always went back home out of pity for her mother, who had developed a serious alcohol problem. The mother herself had grown up in a chaotic family, where the father had died young and her own mother was continuously abusing alcohol.

Besides these chaotic families, there exists also a smaller group of families that present as "model families." These are often "closed" families with a strong parental protection (mostly the mother's) toward the children and little contact with the outside world. The father is usually described as absent and having a peripheral position in the family. Tight, rigid rules exist within the family, and "grandiose," perfectionistic achievements are expected from the children. The bulimic daughter, for example, might be expected to achieve the father's unfulfilled ambition and dream: to obtain a university degree. In these families the tension is often hardly bearable through undiscussable conflicts. However, these mutual conflicts are strongly denied because of loyalty or anxiously concealed on account of the family myth (the "normal" or "ideal" family). Here, the bulimia is often a way to revolt against and, at the same time, to be part of the family system.

> Cathy, 22 years old, had developed a severe bulimia about 5 years earlier, when she left her family to live in a university town. The

family presents itself as decent and exemplary, and laments only the daughter's binges. Apart from that, there is no problem whatsoever, although the mother does have regular migraines and the father three times had had heart problems caused by overwork. Until the age of 18, Cathy was extremely protected by her parents, who constantly forced her to study and pursue a perfectionistic ideal. At the age of 13 and as eldest son, the father had lost his father in World War II and still can not talk about this loss. Within the family, there is no possibility for expressing grief, weakness, or anger. Cathy always has to look good-humored, like the "perfect" daughter. "It's such a pity these binges exist . . ."

In addition to the functional analysis of the family system, the therapist should also thoroughly deal with the *psychosocial functioning of the individual family members*. One must be aware of the often considerable retardation in the patient's personal development because of the entanglement in the bulimic symptomatology. Also, the presence of severe pathology in other family members should be detected. In families of BN patients, mood disorders and substance abuse are often to be found in one or both parents. Some parents might have been severely traumatized themselves in their childhood or youth (e.g., premature death of a family member), might have been witnesses/victims of substance abuse in their own parents, or might have suffered from affective neglect or incest.

The family therapist will then bring all this information together, so as to address the pivotal issue: if and to what extent the symptomatology of the identified patient is interwoven within a dysfunctional family system and continues to play an important role in it. The bulimia may thus have various significances:

- It can act as a lightning conductor for serious marital difficulties or unexpressed sorrow within the family.
- It may signal that the patient was assigned a parental task (parentification), often the case in single-parent families.

- It may be the only way to express aggression and anger within the family.
- It may be the only way to express both the desire and the fear of the patient about developing a more independent attitude toward his or her parents.
- It may be a signal of serious boundary exceeding (incest, aggression) within the family, with traumatic consequences for the patient.
- It may be a way of expressing fear of intimacy and sexual contact.

When the functional analysis does indeed reveal that the bulimia plays a particular role or has a special function in the family system, the therapist will try to develop a working hypothesis wherein the eating problem is connected with the family interaction. The bulimia is then "relabeled" into terms of a resolvable family problem.

> In Myriam's case, the therapist reformulated the BN as follows: "Through the bulimia, Myriam seems to be wishing to make it clear that particular rules and agreements should be adopted in your family. It seems to be her way to ask for change, a need for more freedom and independence. The bulimia is also a kind of 'problem child' and thus seems to have helped you [parents] to better accept the pain and sorrow about the leaving of your other daughter. Finally, we presume that Myriam's binges also have something to do with her fear of detaching herself from the family."

Another sort of reformulation we often use, especially in couples, is the following. The binges and weight fluctuations are redefined as a signal, a message of the patient's "subconscious" about her relationship with her partner. Through the eating problem the patient expresses in an indirect way something that is already strongly sensed unconsciously, but that the patient dares not yet put consciously into words. Thus, the bingeing is a "silent" message about the relationship, addressed to the partner. In the therapy sessions, they can figure out together the content and meaning of that "unconscious message." Of possible significance are the following:

- I do not love you anymore.
- I am angry with you.
- I do not want to make love with you anymore.
- I am your child rather than your woman.
- You suffocate me, I cannot be myself.

Starting from such reformulations, concrete objectives for change can be discussed and defined with the family or the partner.

MIDDLE PHASE: PROMOTING SEPARATION-INDIVIDUATION

As soon as the therapist has the feeling that a working alliance has been built up with the family, and that the family and patient fully realize the gravity of the symptomatology, the family therapist will adopt a more directive and active attitude. An important pitfall often lurks in the initial phase of the treatment: namely, the immediate compliance with the family's request for change without previously testing the ambivalence toward change. As soon as they realize the gravity of the issue, many families display an almost "bulimic" request for help from the family therapist.

> Helen's parents were deeply disturbed after the first two family sessions. They told us that the problem had to be solved once and for all, and that they were ready to follow—almost blindly—all advice and suggestions of the therapist. They assailed us with many questions, mainly about how the bulimia could be stopped.

Experience has taught us that many BN families show a rather ambivalent attitude toward actual change. They are somewhat afraid of the concrete results or the radical consequences of the therapy.

In this phase of the treatment, therefore, top priority is given to the exploration of and confrontation with this *ambivalence*. By adopting a skeptical attitude and putting the question whether the family can cope with a radical change, we attempt to reflect the ambivalent attitude of the family toward change.

In a particular family, the therapist expressed this as follows: "We would like to help you, but we fear that you may not be ready as yet to cope with the consequences of a change. I mean, for instance, that you [parents] may not be able to let your daughter go her own way. It could also happen that, if your daughter becomes more independent and leaves home, certain tensions would arise in the marital relationship, which you may prefer to keep secret. As to you, Madam [to the mother], I fear that you might become seriously depressed."

In this manner the family therapist attempts to induce the family and the identified patient to reflect upon the possible consequences when the eating problems cease to exist. Once the family therapist and the family have a clear view of their possible ambivalence about change, the therapist can comply more directly with the family's request for change. In an initial phase this means that the family members are often involved in the treatment as *cotherapists*. Although it is a general rule that the responsibility for the eating pattern is assigned completely to the patient—who alone is responsible for the eating (or bingeing)—we are sometimes obliged to ask the question whether the family should not set limits as well.

Mary is 23 years old and has had a persistent BN for 5 years. She lives with her parents, who run a restaurant. At night, Mary devours at her discretion the food stocks of the restaurant, rendering large quantities of food unfit for use by taking a bite here and there. The next morning, her parents find a heap of debris in the kitchen and repeatedly have to buy new food supplies (see the "Case Example" below for further elaboration of this case).

In such situations, the family therapist should first encourage the parents (or partner) to take concrete steps for gradually reducing the binges and gaining some control of certain negative (e.g., financial) consequences. Here are a few examples:

- Parents can be asked to lock the kitchen each night.
- The patient has to pay for all the food consumed through the bulimia.
- Vomiting in the toilet or bathroom is forbidden; the patient must use a special bucket and clean it afterward.

Most families have unrealistic expectations—often reflecting their perfectionist ideal—with regard to the bulimia. They expect their child to stop bingeing all at once, which is impossible and often also undesirable. This is explained to the family and the following agreements can be made. The patient is allowed to binge three times a week, but this has to be confined to only one type of food the patient does not particularly like. The principle of gradually regaining control of the eating pattern (see Chapter 4) is explained to the family. As soon as the patient appears to be capable of gaining somewhat more control over the eating pattern—often with ups and downs—the focus in the family therapy will be gradually shifted from the eating problem to the launching of their child. Most patients who have been living on their own for several years also continue to maintain a strong loyalty tie with their families, though often interwoven with unexpressed aggression.

The principal objectives in this middle phase are, consequently, concentrated on the *separation-individuation process* of the patient with regard to the family of origin. This is obviously connected with the age of these patients, which on average varies from 18 to 25 years. As already mentioned, our follow-up study (Vanderlinden & Vandereycken, 1987) has demonstrated that patients who actually leave the family home and start living independently (or in a foster family or halfway home) function better than patients who stay at their parents' home. These follow-up data are also communicated to the parents in order to motivate them to support their child in separating from the family. Especially in younger BN patients, this proposal to leave the family home, even partially (e.g., to go to a boarding school during the week), can provoke a lot of resistance in the parents ("What is wrong with us?").

> Judith's parents felt offended, even hurt, when in the family sessions we brought up the suggestion of a boarding school. They felt accused, because in their eyes this proposal again confirmed that they had indeed not been good parents, that they were to blame for all the problems.

The family therapist should therefore bring up such a proposal extremely carefully and prepare the family for it thoroughly. Time upon time we try to explain to the parents that, in our opinion and experience, the chances of acquiring and developing autonomy are largely outside of the family home rather than when the child stays at home. Even when the parents intend not to intervene anymore, the environment of the family home itself will continue offering the patient protection and dependence, which may inhibit independence and autonomy.

On the other hand, we have learned that every step made by the patient that is not supported by the parents implies a greater chance of failing. Consequently, the parents should be directly involved in the concrete elaboration of the planning of their child's launching. This may be done by having both the parents and the child look for a rented room, boarding school, or foster family. We have repeatedly tried out the formula of the foster family, especially in younger BN patients (in the age group of 16 to 18 years), but this always meets with at least two practical problems. First, there often is a strong resistance in the parents, and second, there are very few applicant foster families. We have mentioned earlier that hospitalization is indicated especially in multisymptomatic BN (see

Chapter 3)—that is, those patients who, in addition to the bulimia, show other impulsive behaviors (self-mutilation, stealing, promiscuity, alcohol abuse, etc.). Hospitalization also seems indicated sometimes as a first step in the reduction of the patient's dependence on the family. The admission to the group climate of a clinical setting can then be labeled as a stay in a sort of "big foster family" to prepare patients for living on their own.

When the therapist feels that the family does not follow the advice, does not fulfill the tasks, and hence sabotages treatment, the therapeutic strategy will become more indirect. We already mentioned, for instance, the skeptical attitude toward the changes desired by the family. In practice, the therapeutic strategy varies continually: We can adopt an actively confronting attitude, in which at times the family is directly encouraged to make changes (*the direct approach*), whereas at other times the family is restrained and warned against the possible dangers and consequences of the desired changes (*the indirect approach*; Papp, 1983). Indeed, we regularly observe that parents become depressed when their child takes first steps toward living independently. The patient also often relapses into the well-known symptomatology as an expression of fear of the increased independence.

> Dorothy has been living in an apartment for 1 week and states in her diary that she has started bingeing and vomiting every day again. She feels depressed and regularly thinks about suicide. Her parents call us up in panic, asking if Dorothy is really "ready" to plan this important step. "Shouldn't we help our daughter anymore?" they ask us.

In these moments, there exists indeed an actual danger that the parents interpret their daughter's relapse into the bulimic symptoms as evidence that she is not prepared to start living on her own. In almost all families we therefore *predict this relapse*, and/or problems of adaptation in one or both parents, when the child's autonomy increases. In order to avoid this risk but at the same time promote separation from home, treatment in a day center may be a valuable alternative (Vandereycken & Meermann, 1984; Piran & Kaplan, 1990).

In individual and group treatment (see Chapters 4 and 5), emphasis is repeatedly laid on the presence of unrealistic perceptions in these patients as to their body and self-image, and on the importance of questioning and correcting these misperceptions and beliefs (e.g., by means of cognitive restructuring techniques). In our experience with families, we often observe how particular and specific thoughts and beliefs are indirectly suggested or enhanced by parents or other family members.

> Bea is described as a peculiar child, who has always been difficult, dependent, and stubborn. Even now she is perceived as weakish: She studies with difficulty and continually quarrels with everybody. Fortunately, she still has her parents, who are always getting her out of trouble . . .

These messages of being weak, helpless, or incompetent are subtly sent to the identified patient by parents and/or family members. The outside world is perceived as dangerous and threatening, so that the family remains the only rescue. The family therapist should detect these *negative messages*, often given as indirect suggestions, bring them into the open, and reformulate them in the family sessions. As long as the parents perceive their child as weak and unable to change, they will continue protecting the child.

As mentioned, about 45% of our BN patients appear to have gone through severe *traumatic experiences* in their childhood and early youth (sexual and/or physical abuse, parental rejection, involvement in serious marital discord). These events are mostly anxiously concealed by the whole family, wherein every member has been directly or indirectly forbidden to talk about this. Not infrequently these traumatic experiences are repressed or dissociated from the conscious mind. The family therapist should carefully detect possible traumatic events and first talk these over with the patient (see Chapter 6). If these events (e.g., incest) also took place shortly before or during the treatment, providing a maximum of protection for the patient deserves top priority. The patient's hospitalization or removal from home then may be indicated. Legal action should be taken only in emergency situations. Experience has taught us that legal procedures often cause additional trauma and guilt for the patient involved.

FINAL PHASE: ENSURING LONG-TERM CHANGES

Providing and planning a *long-lasting aftercare* constitutes in our opinion the cornerstone for the long-term success of treatment. For the family therapist this implies, among other things, reducing the contact with the family only gradually and being available to the patient and the family for an extended period of time. In this ultimate phase, separate sessions are often held with the patient together with the siblings on the one hand and the parents on the other. An elder brother or sister can be involved to further stimulate the patient's search for autonomy. After discharge, the hospitalized patient is referred to the weekly outpatient group therapy (see Chapter 5). Follow-up assessments (interview and/or questionnaire) are systematically planned after 6 months, and after 1, 2, and 5 years (see Chapter 9).

Clinical experience and our ongoing follow-up study have taught us that improvement rarely happens suddenly; bulimic patients often show periodic remissions and relapses. It is, therefore, naive to expect a spectacular change or "recovery" after only a couple of months. We recommend an aftercare of at least 1 year (after inpatient treatment). If it appears, after many months of efforts, that neither the patient nor the family is motivated to change and that they keep sabotaging every therapeutic attempt, the therapist must have the courage to *refuse further treatment*. We then give them the message that the family has convinced us that our approach may not have been adequate or that the family needs the problems to be prepared for worse.

Final Considerations

Most of the actual treatments of BN are still too individually oriented and pay too little attention to the possible meaning and function of the eating symptoms within a broader psychosocial context, and the family system in particular. Although few therapists have had sufficient long-term intensive experience in working with these families, clinical experience has taught us that this line of approach can be meaningful and effective. The bulimia indeed often implies a relational message or signal. Nevertheless, we have learned that the therapist should proceed with extreme care and that a confronting family therapeutic approach is contraindicated in the following situations (Vandereycken et al., 1989):

- Patients with a long history of eating disorders (more than 10 years) and a significant delay in psychosocial development
- Single-parent and/or broken homes
- Families in which one or both parents display severe psychopathology
- Families with a history of physical or sexual abuse
- Families in which previous family therapeutic attempts have failed

We realize that we neither possess solid facts or data to give this argument more evidential value, nor know when family therapy is indicated. We are convinced, however, that a family-oriented approach, as advocated in the treatment of anorexia nervosa, must also become a basic therapeutic component in a multidimensional treatment for BN.

CASE EXAMPLE

This is the story of Mary, a 23-year-old student, who still lives with her parents. We received a phone call from her mother, asking us in a panic if she could come at once about a problem with her daughter, Mary, who was "carrying on like a wild animal at home, devouring anything edible." An appointment was made for the next day with the whole family. Initially, Mary was hospitalized for a short time (2 months) in the inpatient treatment program because of the seriousness and duration of the bulimia and the intolerable familial situation. After that, the treatment consisting of weekly group therapy combined with family therapy sessions was continued on an outpatient basis. In the following part we shall expound the principal family therapeutic interventions.

Background

As a child, Mary had always been a silent but good daughter, both at home and at school. She never had any playmates; she found that studying was more important. At the age of 17 or 18, when she went to college after high school, her character began to change suddenly. She started bingeing, and afterward also vomiting and purging. Mary managed to conceal these problems for several years to all the other family members, although her mother sometimes smelled something in the toilet or noticed that candy was disappearing. About 1 year ago, Mary was caught vomiting in the toilet by her mother. After that, intolerable tensions and conflicts arose in the family. Family members tried to stop Mary's bingeing and vomiting either gently or harshly, but in vain. The more the family interfered with her problems, the more violently she resisted and the more persistent the bingeing-vomiting-purging cycle became. The family doctor and a psychiatrist were consulted. Appetite suppressants and tranquilizers were prescribed, but these did not bring about the slightest change. The mother was given the address of our center by a friend and, at her wits' end, she made an appointment with us.

It was the mother who immediately started the conversation. All the problems were caused by Mary, who, "I really don't know for how long," according to the mother, "has binged secretly during the day and in the past months even at night." Last week Mary had even forced a window and a door, which is locked each night, before bedtime, to get into the kitchen. The next morning, the parents found ruin in the kitchen. Since they were restaurant keepers, the situation at home was no longer tolerable. Every week, Mary ruined a considerable amount of food, and in the mornings, after discovery of the battlefield in his kitchen, the father often had to go out to hurriedly buy new food supplies.

Mary, who sat between both parents, was still and reticent. She was the only daughter (23 years old) and had one younger brother (Frank, 20 years old) and one elder brother (Michael, 25 years old). The father and both sons endorsed the mother's statement. The grandfather (on mother's side) also lived at home and was chef de cuisine. He did not want to come along "because he did not have anything to do with his granddaughter's problem anyway." On further examination of the bulimic problem, it appeared that Mary also vomited each day and used laxatives, sometimes up to 50 pills per day.

The family was at their wits' end. Everybody—except Mary—found that they had tried everything possible. At night they locked the kitchen, but this did not help either, as Mary had already "burgled" her way in twice in the past week. The parents could no longer sleep, and to prevent an even worse situation, just left all the doors open again.

Assessment of the Family System

The first step is the assessment of the family system, wherein the drawing of a *family genogram* may be very useful (see Figure 5). It strikes us that both parents had been confronted with the premature loss of a family member in their families of origin. The mother's mother died in a bombardment in World War II. The mother, then at the age of 12 and eldest daughter, was prematurely delegated the task of mother (parentified). She always felt lonely and misunderstood, was not given a chance to study, and even now is very unhappy about this. The father's family of origin had been seriously shocked by the death of the eldest son (18 years old) in a car crash. They had never talked about this loss at home, and everybody had mourned in silence. After this loss, an atmosphere of bitterness had reigned in the family and the father's parents had begun to overprotect their children. When Mary's parents married, the young couple moved into the mother's parental house and so

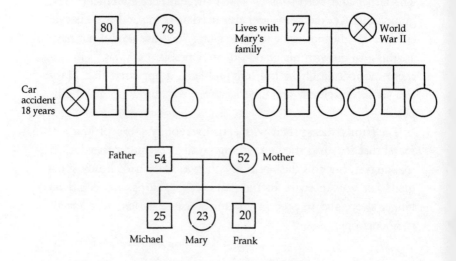

Figure 5. Family Genogram.

lived with the grandfather. From a separate interview with the parents, it later appeared that the father had always had the feeling that his wife was closer to her own father than to himself. Mary's father had always felt secondary to his father-in-law. Mary's family finds itself in an *important transitional phase in the life cycle*: The children have grown to be young adults and will all shortly leave the family home. This separation process leads to many tensions and conflicts, which remain undiscussed. Both parents find little support in each other; it seems as though they are afraid to have to function again as a couple (husband and wife) without children.

When we look at the *familial structure*, it seems as though the mother has a coalition with her own father, while her husband has a secret coalition with Mary. The relationship between the parents is businesslike, cool, and superficial. Both brothers are rather carefully and unconspicuously detaching themselves from the family. Roughly, the familial structure appears tightly and rigidly bounded against the outside world, whereas within the family, boundaries between the different generations and subsystems (grandfather, parents, children) are lacking. The family members feel angry, helpless, and desperate about Mary's bingeing and vomiting; they think that it is a lack of willpower and perseverance. A marked aggressive atmosphere reigns in the family: The mother and daughter have been fighting regularly in the past weeks; they have been throwing plates and food, and only the grandfather's intervention could calm them down.

Assessment of the Individual System

Both parents still have difficulties in dealing with the nasty events they had experienced in their families of origin. The mother drinks regularly, but her alcohol problem is strongly denied by everyone. The father has already had two coronaries, which he also considers to be of "secondary" importance. At certain times he takes to drinking as well. Mary's brothers seem to have few social contacts. They rarely go out and neither of them has ever had a girlfriend. They devote themselves almost exclusively to studying. Mary also is still extremely dependent on her family: Apart from studying she does not have a single hobby or interest. Social contacts have always been strongly avoided.

Provisional Working Hypothesis

After a few sessions, the following considerations are carefully presented to the family: "It seems to us that Mary's bulimia may signal in your family that significant alterations and adaptations should take place in your relationships with one another. We understand that you, parents, considering the experiences in your families of origin, are extremely concerned about the fate and future of your children, who have meanwhile become young adults. This is an age when most youths start flying out of the nest. Mary's bulimia may well signify a need for more freedom and autonomy, or she may rather express her fear of detaching herself from the family and stepping into the outside world. Moreover, we are wondering if you [parents] are prepared to detach yourselves from your daughter and both your sons, so that they may start living their own lives." The family responded partly with approval and partly with confusion. The parents, especially, did not quite understand why they should have problems if their daughter would start living elsewhere. To them, the problem was that "Mary may be unable to live on her own and is certainly not prepared for it."

Constructing Intergenerational Boundaries

After a few weeks Mary very carefully puts forward other problems in the group therapy sessions: Both her parents regularly have screaming rows and separately resort to alcohol abuse. Her father then refuses to sleep with her mother and spends the night in bed with Mary. She always lets him have his way, but feels extremely tense and anxious whenever he sleeps with her. Mary explicitly requests that we never discuss this topic in the family sessions, as her father would never forgive her. These new data are immediately discussed in the therapeutic team: The presumption of far-reaching boundary exceeding (possibly incest) together with severe marital discord and alcohol abuse is confirmed. The team proposes to persuade Mary to discuss these problems in the family sessions after all: Clear agreements should be made as to her ceasing her involvement in the marital disputes between the parents. Arrangements should also be made to stop the father from sleeping with his daughter. Mary hesitatingly approves. It is then agreed to first arrange a session with both her brothers, in the hope that they may support her in the next family session. The conversation with the brothers is rather difficult. They too are afraid to discuss the drinking problem and the boundary exceeding with their parents. During this session the bulimia is reformulated as Mary's way to utter her anger and anxiety regarding the family problems. It is agreed that the family therapist will first have a separate interview with the parents.

In the following session we notice that both parents are very tense. They state that they almost never talk together. "We haven't time, we are completely absorbed in our work," the father tells us. Both parents do admit that marital disputes occasionally occur and that they seldom have sexual contact ("My wife is mostly not in the mood, she rejects me"), but they both minimize this problem. The family therapist prefers, for the time being, considering the resistance in both parents, not to explore more deeply the marital problems. However, he decides to discuss the serious boundary exceeding and makes it clear that both parents should make sure that the father no longer sleeps with his daughter. As these parents tend to shirk their responsibility, the therapist attempts to convey to both parents the feeling that in so doing they make a serious mistake and may well feel guilty about this. When the father is asked whether he had not gone too far with his daughter, he first begins to blush, then at once gets angry and shouts at the top of his lungs: "Has Mary been telling you any stories?" At that moment, the mother comes to his aid and reluctantly admits that she has indeed refused to have sex with her husband for many years. She starts crying and tells us how she never had the feeling herself of being loved by her parents and how difficult it is for her to give love herself. She tells us how badly she wishes every week her mother were still alive and how she silently mourns over her. Father is astounded; he was totally unaware of this. Another session is planned with the parents to talk more about the deceased mother.

By placement of the issue in an *intergenerational context*, a new entrance into the therapeutic process seems to have been created. In the following session with the parents it comes out that the mother has not visited the tomb of her deceased mother for years, in spite of the fact that they live close to the cemetery. They accept our proposal that they pay a visit to the churchyard together, in which the father will try to support and console his wife. During this session, both parents also state that it would probably be better for Mary if her father no longer slept with her. They are also willing to communicate this to her. This takes place in the following family session. Mary is now able to put into words her intense feelings of anxiety about her father's sleeping with her at night. For the very first time the parents admit to their children that they have problems in their relationship and that they are ready to do something about it. Although everybody seems to be somewhat relieved, the tension in the family increases strikingly after this session.

Promoting Independence

As Mary has gained some control over her bulimic urge and will soon stop the inpatient treatment, it is decided in the team to put the focus on the launching from the family. Both Mary and her parents had already raised the suggestion of her starting to live on her own. But when the therapist raises this suggestion in the family sessions, all kinds of objections are put forward: "Mary would never manage this, she is not yet ripe for it." Moreover, the grandfather believes that it is unbecoming for such a young lady to start living on her own. It is then again urgently requested to bring the grandfather along to the following family session, which finally happens.

The grandfather is a very grumpy and embittered man, coming along very reluctantly. He fails to see why Mary has been hospitalized for a problem that can be solved simply by a little bit of willpower. The family is then asked to expound Mary's problems to her grandfather, while the family therapist underlines the importance and usefulness of his granddaughter's living on her own. As the conversation progresses, the grandfather becomes more open and compliant, especially after his own account of his misery after the death of his wife and about the support received from his children. As "a kind of experiment," the family finally assents to the proposal of Mary's living independently. Everyone is then warned that Mary will have a very difficult start. A relapse into the bulimic symptoms is predicted as an often inevitable step in the therapeutic process.

Aftercare

Mary finds a room in a student home and furnishes this to her own liking with the help of her parents and her brothers. After about 2 months the inpatient treatment is terminated, and Mary then attends the weekly outpatient group therapy for bulimic patients. The family is also given further therapeutic guidance (once a month). Mary very soon relapses into daily bingeing and vomiting: She feels lonely, depressed, and sometimes suicidal. She is requested not to discuss this with her parents; nevertheless, she calls them up in panic, telling them that she is desperate and wants to go back home. Fortunately, her parents have meanwhile learned that everybody is better off if Mary keeps living on her own; things are more peaceful at home and they can at last eat without quarreling again. With the support of the family therapist, they manage to persuade Mary to keep on trying. Also in the group therapy, she is encouraged to keep it up. After this acute relapse, things gradually go better.

As soon as the episodes of bulimia have decreased (to about once a week), other themes are brought up in the group therapy, such as starting a relationship, falling in love, sexuality, dealing with conflicts, learning to trust others. After about 6 months (following the completion of the inpatient treatment), the family therapy evolves toward separate sessions with husband and wife, while Mary further discusses her problems in group therapy. Only then can the marital issue be gone into in more depth, however without much success. The alcohol abuse decreases somewhat, but both parents regularly (at least once a week) keep resorting to alcohol. They both trivialize this problem. It is also remarkable how Mary's bulimia reemerges whenever the marital tensions increase. Husband and wife do not seem to manage to screen off their relationship against the grandfather's interference. Finally, after about 1 year, they stop the treatment themselves. Mary continues to attend the outpatient group therapy for 2 years.

At follow-up, 1 year later, she is living with a boyfriend, and functioning fairly well. Though sporadically (once in 2 months) she has a binge, she does not worry about this. Her weight remains stable. Meanwhile, her parents keep on drinking and quarreling. "But that's their business. After all it's their life," Mary says, "I live my own now!"

8

Inpatient Treatment

The description of a specialized inpatient treatment for eating disorders is outside the scope of this book. Other authors have reported on this subject in detail (e.g., Andersen, 1985; Piran & Kaplan, 1990; Wooley & Wooley, 1985). We shall confine ourselves to a few main lines of the approach in the University Psychiatric Center at Kortenberg, Belgium (for details, see Vandereycken, 1985; 1987c, 1988; Vandereycken & Meermann, 1984).

DECISION AND PREPARATION FOR ADMISSION

In Chapter 3 we briefly discussed possible indications for inpatient treatment of BN. We summarize the principal criteria for hospitalization as follows:

- Critical physical condition
- Risk of suicide
- Multisymptomatic BN
- Intolerable familial situation
- Extreme social isolation
- Failure of outpatient treatment

As a general rule it should be established that a long-lasting hospitalization is in most cases contraindicated. Most BN patients, once admitted to the protective and structured environment of a hospital setting, appear to be able to stop very soon the bingeing-vomiting-purging cycle. As in other addictions, this "success" is misleading. After discharge, many patients soon relapse into the disturbed eating behavior. Therefore, during the inpatient treatment, it should be ensured that the patients are regularly confronted with the outside world. In our center this is done by having the patient, after a period of adaptation of 3 weeks (a sort of "detoxification"), plan activities at fixed times outside the psychiatric center. If possible, we also prefer to have the final phase of the treatment in a day hospital (see also Piran & Kaplan, 1990). An admission to a psychiatric center is regarded by many—patient, family and/or partner, referring authority—as the ultimate solution. But delaying this decision might be unjust as well. A short-term admission is sometimes the only way to break through the vicious circle of bingeing-vomiting-purging and to bend it into a constructive therapeutic commitment.

The motivation of both patient and family (or partner) is the first step and a basic requirement for a favorable course of inpatient treatment (see also Chapter 7). In principle, no patient will be hospitalized without the explicit consent of the parents and/or partner. We have learned that an intensive therapeutic alliance with the family and/or partner is a conditio sine qua non to render the hospitalization meaningful and effective (Vandereycken, 1987b). Before admission, the family—or at least the parents (or partner)—should therefore always be invited to a session and thoroughly informed about the seriousness of the issue, the purpose of the hospitalization, the necessity of their cooperation, and the importance of long-lasting aftercare.

When the therapist considers that an admission is indicated, and proposes this to the patient and family, the following reactions may occur. First, there are patients and parents who react with anger and radically refuse the hospitalization as though it were an offense or a punishment. The outpatient treatment is then often terminated. It regularly occurs that these patients report again for admission a few months or even years later, after the umpteenth failed attempt at therapy elsewhere. A second but large group assents to the admission after long consideration and hesitation. Patient and/or family will then start the inpatient treatment with rather ambivalent feelings. A third group is relieved by the possibility of breaking through a disastrous behavioral pattern. When the decision for hospitalization has been made, this often means that those deciding are sufficiently aware of the seriousness of the issue. A fourth (though small) group seizes all too eagerly the proposal of an admission. Here exists the danger of their regarding the hospital as a sort of refuge or of expecting a miraculous cure.

In the initial phase of inpatient treatment, the normalization of the eating pattern (ceasing of the bingeing-vomiting-purging cycle) is of primordial importance. The main accent of the treatment will then be gradually laid on the significance of the bulimia, the search for adequate alternatives to the binges, and the planning of actual changes on both individual and interactional levels. At admission, the patients themselves are thoroughly informed about the general principles, directives, and agreements during their hospitalization. A treatment plan is offered to them in the way of a contract. Also, the family is given a special information brochure (see Vandereycken et al., 1989).

TREATMENT CONTRACT

In the following paragraphs we will present the treatment contract, such as it is offered to the patient. The contract is quite similar to the one we use with anorexia nervosa patients (both types of patients are mixed in our inpatient groups). The central idea is to gradually delegate more responsibilities and liberties to patients, as they prove to be capable of assuming these.

A. General principles and guidelines

We wish to inform you about the general guidelines and rules of our treatment program. It concerns the main rules we refer to for any decisions and agreements during your stay in our center. Naturally, we shall reckon with individual differences and adapt any form of therapy according to your personal situation and the objectives of your treatment. Treatment will be focused in the first place on restoring a normal eating pattern and, if needed, also a normal weight. To achieve this, we have worked out a treatment plan that will allow you relative freedom on the one hand, but that also comprises certain conditions on the other. Only after it appears that you are unable to deal with the freedom allowed according to our agreements shall we temporarily take over the control, depending on your evolution and according to the agreements expounded below. The final treatment goals are concretely agreed upon with you, but we set forward some basic therapeutic requirements. This means, among other things, that a "normal" or *target weight* is established, based on scientific data. All decisions that form the basis of this program are made in the team meeting.

The treatment is divided into three phases.

First phase: a minimum of 3 weeks, the main purpose being the stabilization of weight and normalization of eating behavior.

Second phase: stabilization of a normal eating pattern or, if needed, the period until half of the provided weight adaptation is reached.

Third phase: reorientation to adaptation in the outside world and, if needed, the period until the target weight is reached.

If the body weight is already normalized, the second and third phases will last at least 3 weeks. Whoever has normalized weight in the second phase can perform the third phase in day treatment (on the same ward). The course in phases is a crucial element in the treatment. The transition from one phase to another, however, is not exclusively determined on the basis of eating behavior or weight change. The psychological aspects and involvement in different therapeutic activities are also rated in the evaluation. Each month, your evolution will be evaluated by yourself, the other group members, and the team.

B. Basic rules

During the first phase, the weight must remain stable (no fluctuations of more than 4 lb per week). According to special arrangements with the team, bingeing, vomiting, and/or purging should be kept under control as soon as possible. If necessary, the first phase (a minimum of 3 weeks) may be prolonged in mutual agreement with the team. If a weight increase is required during the second and third phases, a weekly increase of 1 lb will be expected, counting from the first week of your second phase. When you remain under the minimum weight limit for 3 weeks on end, exception program 1 (in phase 1) or 2 (in phase 2) will be applied until the minimum limit is reached again. Weight fluctuations should not amount to more than 3 lb with regard to the previous control. If you do not answer these conditions, exception program 2 (in phase 2) or 3 (in phase 3) will be applied for 5 days. If a weight decrease is required during the second and third phases, individual limits will be agreed upon and a diet will be arranged for you.

It is not allowed to eat or nibble between meals, or to keep food in your room. During the first and second phases, it is also compulsory to stay for at least 1 hour in the common livingroom after each meal. In case of repeated difficulties (for instance, very frequent vomiting or bingeing), an exception program will also be applied (respectively 1, 2, or 3, according to the phase of treatment in which you find yourself at that time). During the treatment, you will keep a diary, which will be discussed once a week with the group nurse.

C. Rules in the regular program

First phase

- You have your meals in the refectory, attended by a nurse. You are given a fixed portion; any other food or candy is not permitted. For supper, however, you are given a dessert as an extra, which you may consume in the course of the evening (before 9 P.M.).
- You are weighed each day after breakfast.
- You may receive visitors on Saturdays and Sundays.
- An adaptation period of 3 weeks is provided. During this period you shall remain on the ward and may leave this only for medical examinations, psychological tests, and therapies. After the first 3 weeks, you may leave the ward with visitors, after agreement with the nurse.
- Writing and receiving letters are not permitted during the first 3 weeks. Telephone calls are restricted to one on the weekend.
- It is forbidden to enter the kitchen, except for planned activities.

Second phase

- You have your meals in the refectory, attended by a nurse. You are given a fixed portion; any other food or candy is not permitted.
- You are weighed after breakfast three times a week.
- You may leave the ward according to the general rules.
- Telephone calls and correspondence by letter are permitted.
- You can receive visitors both on Saturdays and Sundays. During the weekend you may leave the hospital with visitors one afternoon. Meals, however, must be taken in the hospital.
- There is opportunity to go on an outing after agreement with the team. You have the opportunity to organize an

activity outside the hospital with group members of the second and third phase.

- It is forbidden to enter the kitchen, except for planned activities.

Third phase

- You have your meals in the refectory, and you make your food choice for yourself.
- You are weighed twice a week.
- You can receive visitors every day according to the rules of the section.
- You may leave the hospital for an activity in the neighborhood or to spend the weekend elsewhere, according to the general rules of the ward. If possible, you can have this phase in the form of day hospital treatment.
- You are considered for the task of group leader.

D. Rules in the exception program

Exception program 1

- You have your meals in the refectory with fixed portions, attended by a nurse.
- You are weighed every day after breakfast.
- You wear nightclothes and stay in your room, except for therapies and leisure hours (10–11 A.M., 4–5 P.M., 7:30–8:30 P.M.
- A 1-hour visit is permitted either on Saturdays or on Sundays.
- You may make one phone call on the weekend, after agreement with the team.
- It is not permitted to enter either the kitchen or the refectory.

Exception program 2

- You have your meals in the refectory with fixed portions and attended by a nurse.

- You are weighed three times per week.
- You wear normal clothes and stay in your room, except for therapies and leisure hours (10–11 A.M., 4–5 P.M., and 7:30–8:30 P.M.; on Saturdays and Sundays, in addition, from 9 to 10 A.M. and from 1:30 to 2:30 P.M.).
- You may make two phone calls during the week and one on the weekend, after agreement with the team.
- You may write and receive two letters per week.
- You are allowed 2 hours' visit either on Saturdays or on Sundays.
- It is not permitted to enter the kitchen.

Exception program 3

- You have your meals in the refectory attended by a nurse, and you make your own food choice.
- You are weighed twice a week.
- You may make three phone calls per week and only on the weekend upon agreement with the team.
- You may write and receive three letters per week.
- You are allowed 3 hours' visit either on Saturdays or on Sundays.

Special measure

If you have to be integrated into an exception program for 2 successive weeks:

- In program 2 and 3, you are referred to the previous program.
- In program 1, visits, correspondence, and leisure hours outside your room are canceled.

E. Further treatment

The restoration of normal weight and eating behavior is a necessary step to find permanent solutions to the tensions, problems, and conflicts you had to struggle with. Weight or eating is certainly not what matters most in the treatment, but rather your feelings and thoughts, anxieties, or uncertainties about yourself and your relations at home with your family or partner. These aspects are paid special attention in the following ways (you will be given more information about each therapy by the team members): occupational therapy, psychomotor therapy, group psychotherapy, weekly evaluation with the nurse, sex education group, sessions with family and/or partner.

SPECIFIC THERAPEUTIC ACTIVITIES

The treatment contract quoted above functions as a guideline and holds for both team and patient during inpatient treatment. Most bulimic patients often state that such a treatment contract—although they constantly detest it—is exactly what they need, because it offers them structure and regularity, which they are lacking in their daily life. The contract also aims at reducing to an absolute minimum the often endless discussions about eating and weight and about the agreements thereupon, so that the entire attention may be focused on the underlying psychological significance of the bulimia. The Goal Attainment Evaluation is also employed during inpatient treatment (see Chapter 5), because it may guide and coordinate all therapeutic activities for both patient and therapeutic team. The group psychotherapist has an important coordinating function in the treatment. Besides the task within the group psychotherapy, he or she is also the principal therapist for parents, family, and/or partner. It has already been thoroughly expounded (respectively in Chapters 5 and 7) how these functions are concretely carried out.

As for the *guidance of families* (parents/partners), we should mention that this is carried out in different ways during the inpatient treatment: First, all parents are invited to the fortnightly parent counseling group under the guidance of a couple of therapists; apart from this, there also exists a similar partner counseling group. Most families are further seen in separate family or marital therapy sessions. Although the frequency of these sessions obviously depends strongly on both the need and necessity of each separate family, we have learned that it is certainly not necessary to plan weekly family sessions. In practice, we never plan more than one family session every 2 or 3 weeks.

Patients have an *occupational therapy* session every day, where, besides individual creative tasks, a good many group activities are planned around one specific theme. A basic assignment for all patients herein is the portrayal of their families in a drawing, painting, or collage. Role playing and psychodrama techniques are also employed in occupational therapy.

Three times a week, patients also have a *psychomotor therapy* session, which is specifically focused on detecting and correcting disorders in body experience. During this "body-oriented therapy," frequent use is made of mirror exercises and video-confrontation (Vandereycken, 1990b).

Special attention is also paid to sexual knowledge and experience through the *sex education group* under the guidance of a female therapist. With the help of video or reading material, information is given about sexuality and experiences are discussed.

Twice a week (before and after the weekend) the group meets under the *guidance of the group nurse*. Special attention is paid to the concrete execution of the treatment plan and to detailed weekend planning, which is also thoroughly evaluated afterward. Arrangements are agreed upon as to household activities, including a weekly cooking assignment, cleaning of one's own room, and upkeep of the common rooms. Cooking together may teach patients to deal with eating in a different manner again and obviously creates a good many fascinating interactions among the different group members.

In group meetings with the *social worker* all kinds of subjects are thematically brought up (also by the patients themselves): applying for a job, living on one's own, extra education or professional training, social legislation, leisure activities, et cetera.

After discharge from the hospital, BN patients take part in the weekly outpatient group therapy (see Chapter 5). On an average, the patients will be followed up intensively for 6 months to 1 year. Experience has taught us that long-lasting aftercare is of crucial importance for a favorable prognosis, especially in "difficult" BN patients meeting the aforementioned criteria for inpatient treatment.

9

Evaluation and Follow-up

In this last chapter another difficult task remains to be performed: a critical investigation of the state of the art as to the evaluation of treatment effects. Most of the treatments for BN propagated in the literature still are in an experimental stage. Follow-up and controlled research data are extremely scarce. The greatest difficulty in the judgment of treatment effects is the lack of clearly described evaluation criteria.

MULTIDIMENSIONAL EVALUATION

No clear-cut standards or evaluation criteria have as yet been described in the scientific literature that might enable us to evaluate objectively the seriousness and course of BN (for discussion of methodological problems, see Herzog, Deter, & Vandereycken, 1992). Moreover, most studies are nearly exclusively based on an evaluation of the symptomatic level: the presence or absence of bingeing, vomiting, and purging after a certain period of treatment. Herein, figures and percentages can often be misleading: A decrease in binge-eating frequency from five times a day to five times a week is actually an improvement of more than 80%, but can hardly be labeled as a cure! Above all, the question whether a cure corresponds to a complete and permanent absence of bingeing remains unanswered for us. And even if the binges remain absent, does this automatically mean that the patients have also succeeded in developing their personal and relational life in a satisfactory way?

Thus, in the evaluation of the effectiveness of therapy programs, not only should the eating pattern be evaluated, but also the other levels: namely, those factors that refer to the behavior and the subjective perception of patients in dealing with themselves and significant others. A thorough evaluation therefore implies a multidimensional assessment. In our center, patients are evaluated systematically at stated times (after 6 months and 1, 2, and 5 years) by means of standardized scales (such as the EDES; see Appendix A) that attempt to evaluate both the symptomatic level and the global psychosocial functioning of the patient. The obtained results apparently remain a subjective account of the patient.

The importance of the relative *absence of binges* is closely connected with the starting point of the therapy: abstinence versus nonabstinence. Since we do not demand that BN patients stop bingeing and vomiting immediately, the abandonment of this eating ritual is a slow process. However, from experience it appears that a number of patients are not capable of stopping completely and continue to live with an isolated symptom. They still binge and/or vomit occasionally (e.g., once a month), without any influence on their psychosocial functioning. On the basis of our experience, we may well question whether these patients are therefore "less" cured than others. After all, presence or absence of binges alone is no guarantee whatsoever of satisfactory changes in one's personal life. Moreover, we are extremely surprised by the fact that an improvement is much too often evaluated as a function of decrease in or absence of eating pathology, and not as a function of presence of a normal eating pattern. The primary question that should be put in an evaluation investigation is therefore: Does the patient again have normal meals each day and can the patient enjoy eating? Afterward, it can be further determined whether the patient still binges, diets, vomits, and/or purges; how frequently; and whether this interferes with her physical and psychosocial functioning.

We wish to emphasize once more that most patients regularly have a revival of binges in the course of their treatment and that we try, time after time, to convince them that this does not mean that they have completely relapsed into the bulimia. The binges are regarded as a signal that patients find themselves in a situation of increased risk, which they cannot cope with at that moment. It is important that they accept that such a relapse remains possible in the future as a sign that earlier solutions to certain problems were superficial and that it is necessary to search further for a satisfactory solution to these problematic situations.

More important than evaluation of the symptomatic level is the evaluation of psychosocial functioning—and it is also much more difficult. Important questions herein are the following:

- Have patients detached themselves somewhat from their family, in the sense that they can live their own life satisfactorily?
- Do patients have at least one significant relationship outside the family?
- Do patients devote sufficient time to social activities and leisure?
- How do patients experience their body and sexuality?

PROGNOSTIC FACTORS

In the literature, the following prognostic factors have been reported:

- Patients who respond very positively to the treatment maintain the improvement over the next 2 years, but even these patients may have isolated episodes of bulimic symptoms (Hsu & Holder, 1986; Pyle, Mitchell, Eckert, Hatsukami, Pomeroy, & Zimmerman, 1990).
- Comorbidity with personality disorders significantly affects outcome in an unfavorable way (Johnson, Tobin, & Dennis,

1990; Glassman, Rich, Darko, & Clarkin, 1990; Fichter, 1992).

- Patients with multi-impulsive BN connected with alcohol and/or drug abuse and self-destructive tendencies often need a long-lasting treatment (Andersen, 1985; Lacey, 1985, 1992).
- A previous history of anorexia nervosa is associated with a poorer prognosis (Lacey, 1983; Wilson, 1989), and these patients tend to react more slowly to treatment (Lacey, 1992).
- The occurrence of alcoholism, eating disorders, or psychiatric disorders in the family often goes along with treatment problems, but the connection with the outcome of the treatment is not yet clear (Hsu & Holder, 1986).
- A good predictor for a positive treatment result is the feeling of self-esteem (Fairburn, 1988) and a positive body image (Wertheim, 1988; Vandereycken, 1990b).

When we relate these factors to our clinical experiences and preliminary results of our own follow-up investigations, we can observe the following.

A *positive response during the first months* of treatment seems indeed to be an important prognostic factor. Thus, we were able to establish that patients who showed no evident change after 3 months of clinical treatment did not change favorably in a long-lasting treatment either. Hence, for a favorable prognosis it seems important that the treatment should have caught on after a few months.

The frequently quoted assumption *the longer the duration of illness, the less favorable the prognosis*, has been partly confirmed by our research data. Yet, we believe this is a dangerous thought for the therapist. From our follow-up investigation in a group of older and chronic patients ($N = 30$) with an average age of 25 years and a duration of illness of 46 months, 55% ($N = 16$) of the patients appeared, 2 years after admission, to function normally on the basis of the EDES score and, moreover, to be able to do without therapy. Another group of eight patients functioned significantly better than before the admission, but still displayed problems. These results seem to clearly demonstrate that the therapist should have good expectations for chronic patients with long duration of illness instead of labeling them lost causes.

The prognosis appears to be rather unfavorable in *multisymptomatic bulimic patients*, who, besides the eating disorder, display other psychiatric problems (e.g., depression, obsessions, self-mutilation, alcohol abuse, post-traumatic stress disorder). An intensive inpatient treatment as a start then seems indicated.

A *history of anorexia nervosa*, especially when this is still present (for instance, weight that is too low), may hamper the treatment. Our clinical experience, however, demonstrates that this should not always be the case.

Our own experience and research indicate that treatment is laborious and prognosis less favorable in *families with severe psychopathology in one or both parents*. Also, the treatment of patients from single-parent families is often quite difficult.

Naturally, a *positive change in the feeling of self-esteem and body perception* will be a favorable prognostic factor. This is confirmed by our investigation. In a large group ($N = 54$), the evaluations of patients themselves (on the basis of their GAE form) were studied at the end of their clinical treatment and as a function of their follow-up results (based on the EDES) 6 months and 1 year after admission. From this, one factor appeared to have an evident prognostic value: Patients who, at completion of the inpatient treatment, evaluated themselves as totally unchanged—who had the feeling that the treatment had brought about not the slightest positive change—all functioned unchanged at follow-up and, thus, without any further positive progress (Vanderlinden & Vandereycken, 1988b).

Mental preoccupation

(none = 6; slight = 4; strong = 2; extreme = 0)
Nutrition   7: _____
Weight   8: _____

Menses

(regular = 6; irregular or with pill = 4; rare = 2;
absent = 0)   9: _____

Sexuality

(pleasure, satisfaction = 6–4–2–0 = aversion, avoidance)
Attitude toward sex   10: _____
Active sex   11: _____

Social adaptation

(good/satisfactory = 6; moderate/varying = 4;
insufficient/weak = 2; bad/absent = 0)
Attitude toward parents   12: _____
Social contacts   13: _____
Study or work   14: _____

General psychological state (apart from eating problems)

6 = normal (compared to peers)
4 = slightly abnormal (for instance: slight psychosomatic
    complaints, slight mood fluctuations; no specific ther-
    apy needed)
2 = obviously disturbed (for instance: anxiety state,
    depression; psychiatric treatment and/or psychother-
    apy necessary)
0 = severely disturbed (for instance: psychosis, addiction,

suicide attempt; intensive therapy or hospitalization
required)   15: ____

Total score (sum 1 to 15)   : ____

Note on scoring and interpretation
A comparative study among 370 eating disorder patients and 174 "normal" women yielded a cutoff score of 55, showing a sensitivity of 93 (7% false negatives above 55) and a specificity of 96 (4% false positives below 55).

If used as an evaluation instrument for repeated assessments, it is advised that one look at changes on the four subscales (based on a factor analytic study):

1. *Anorexic preoccupation* (items 1, 2, 3, 7, and 8).
2. *Bulimic behavior* (items 4, 5, and 6).
3. *Sexuality* (items 9, 10, and 11).
4. *Psychosocial adjustment* (items 12, 13, 14, and 15).

Appendix B

GOAL ATTAINMENT EVALUATION (GAE)
GAE PLAN

Name: Date:

Describe six problem areas, two of each category (A, B, C) that you would like to work on during your treatment. Specify, in each of these therapy goals, at least three possibilities (concrete steps) to achieve this goal.

A. Eating/weight problems

Problem area A1:
      Step (a)
          (b)
          (c)
Problem area A2:
      Step (a)
          (b)
          (c)

B. Self-perception

Problem area B1:
      Step (a)
          (b)
          (c)
Problem area B2:
      Step (a)
          (b)
          (c)

C. Interactions

Problem area C1:
      Step (a)
          (b)
          (c)
Problem area C2:
      Step (a)
          (b)
          (c)

GAE EVALUATION FORM

Patient's name:

Reviewer's name: Date:

Indicate for each problem area to what extent this has changed in the past weeks (since previous evaluation). Base your judgment on the concrete steps indicated for each purpose. Render your judgment by means of a cross on the corresponding evaluation scale.*

Problem area	strongly deteriorated	slightly deteriorated	unchanged	slightly improved	strongly improved	totally solved
A1						
A2						
B1						
B2						
C1						
C2						

---

*When the principle of the "Visual Analogue Scale" is employed, the evaluation (e.g., on a line of 10 cm) can also be transposed into a more precise number, which may facilitate the processing of data and enable comparative investigations.

Appendix C

INFORMATION BROCHURE ABOUT BULIMIA NERVOSA

Bulimia points to an irresistible urge for food (mostly sweets or calorie-rich food) or the feeling of being unable to stop eating. This creates periods of bingeing—rapid consumption of great amounts of food—which, because of the person's fear of growing "fat," are followed by (self-induced) vomiting, laxative abuse, or rigorous fasting, all of these aimed at keeping the weight under control. This disturbed eating behavior arises from and is maintained by a combined action of factors that are closely related to one another. These different factors will first be illustrated in this brochure. After that, a few aspects of the treatment will be discussed.

In Search of Yourself

As one grows up, especially after puberty, one has to take countless new steps in life. There is school, with its increasing demands to perform well and thus prepare for a future profession. There are the relationships within and outside the family, in which one must gradually detach oneself from one's parents and learn to live one's own life. There is the body, which undergoes great changes and takes on new shapes, turning the child into an adult. All these alterations (mostly between the ages of 10 and 20 years) may cause great uncertainty. One has the feeling of no longer being oneself or one is afraid of being unable to deal with this. When one has been used in one's childhood to doing everything as best as one could, one soon notices that this is no longer so simple. Gradually, the inclination to be satisfied only with the best can then arise, which often means that one is never satisfied: School results are never good enough, there is always something wrong with one's physical appearance, and one feels easily inferior to others, as well as more and more lonely and misunderstood. This can cause all kinds of reactions: one withdraws often into oneself, one starts devoting all available time to studying, one wants to have an absolutely perfect body. Especially the latter may then gradually absorb all attention.

Slaves of Fashion

Girls and women especially are under strong pressure to meet the fashionable ideal: Slender is beautiful! Models, movie stars, and pop stars set the "example." This causes the false impression that only slender people are successful, attractive, or loved. However, an investigation has shown that the present cover girls are even more slender than in the past, whereas the average weight of young adult women has increased in the past 30 years! In other words, there arises an ever-growing gap between reality (how I am) and ideal (how I would like to be). Every girls' or women's magazine adroitly takes advantage of this by recommending each month a new sort of miraculous diet. Slenderness thus becomes a product that is sold with a lot of publicity. This strong pressure exerted on women to slenderize can also be found in another fad: fitness. This would be "necessary" to acquire and preserve a beautiful, slender figure. Jogging, aerobics, and other physical exercises thus become new weapons for keeping one's weight under control.

All this results in dissatisfaction in many women about their own bodies, because they do not have and probably will never attain the "ideal figure." A good many women regard themselves as too heavy, although statistically they have a normal weight. Other women, who have an evidently too low weight, refuse to recognize this. Still others wish to undergo operations in order to render their bodies more beautiful. And all that because fashion tells them that "slender is beautiful." How long will you continue being the slave of this fashion?

The Decay of a Food Addict

Rigorous dieting or long fasting increases the urge to eat. The stronger the attempt to keep eating under control, the greater the risk of losing all control one day, and of falling into the other extreme (bingeing). When, at a certain moment, one eats more than the diet allowed, one is strongly inclined to keep on eating: "Now that I've 'sinned,' I may as well keep on eating and especially 'forbidden fruits' (cookies, chocolate, or other sweets)."

Unnatural slenderizing through rigorous diets has radical effects on one's behavior:

- Alterations in emotional life such as dejectedness, irritability, and outbursts of anger
- Social alterations, avoidance of contacts for fear of eating, increased loneliness, loss of sexual desire
- Alterations in thinking such as increasing obsession about food and decreased concentration (problems in studying)
- All kinds of physical alterations, which will be discussed hereafter

All these side effects disappear as soon as the eating behavior is normally balanced again. Whoever does not succeed in this can get into serious trouble, especially when, besides dieting and bingeing, vomiting (throwing up) or the abundant use of laxatives and diuretics (water expellers) also occurs. The dieting-overeating-purging cycle maintains itself.

Purging becomes a method to regain control after a period of overeating. It becomes an automatism: "Oh, I can go on eating for I'll go vomit right away . . ." Some even start eating to be able to vomit! Such a state can bring about far-reaching physical complications (see below). Besides the harmful effects, the overeating also means a serious waste and a financial burden. This can sometimes induce the inclination to steal food or money to gratify the urge to eat, like a drug addict who cannot do without drugs.

The Body Off Balance

Body weight is not something that can be quickly altered with a lot of willpower. Our body attempts to maintain a physiological weight level, a certain equilibrium called "setpoint." In order to achieve this, our body functions like the thermostat of the central heating unit as it provides an unchanged room temperature. Thus, in most people, body weight remains constant: Spontaneously, without their calculating, the balance between energy intake (food) and energy consumption (movement) is kept in equilibrium. The important factors that influence this equilibrium are:

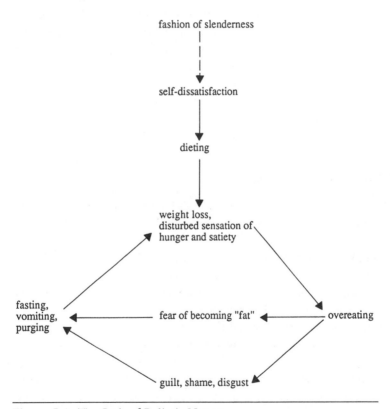

Figure C-1. The Cycle of Bulimia Nervosa.

- Nutrition: Percentage of calories in proportion to normal needs depending on age and stature.
- Exercise: Exercise alone is helpful in stabilization, but not in decrease of body weight.

How does our body respond to a diet? At the start of a diet it is relatively simple to lose a few pounds as a result of loss of fluid. But after that, one reaches a level at which it is difficult to lose weight. In thinning, the body starts "saving" by consuming less. The longer one diets, the more the body resists further loss of weight. Another serious side effect is the disappearance of a normal feeling of hunger and satiation: There is either a constantly gnawing hunger, or, even when eating a lot, one rarely will have the feeling of having had enough. The body is thrown off balance, which is worsened still by overeating and vomiting. The possible physical complications of such an eating behavior are mentioned in Table C-1.

Here, we must mention that laxatives have little influence on weight. Indeed, much nourishment has already been absorbed in the small intestine before a laxative can take effect. The only effect brought about is the feeling of having an "empty" belly.

Steps in the Treatment

The primary condition for treatment is honesty, both with yourself and the therapist. Essential and central in the entire guidance is the keeping of a diary, in which you note everything about your eating behavior: What, how much, where, and when have you eaten? Was there a special occasion? How did you feel before and after eating? and so on. The first phase is aimed at the normalization and stabilization of the eating behavior. The weight is not the central point. The eating pattern takes first place and the weight only second, as the latter is a result of the former. Considering the serious risks, vomiting and purging should cease as soon as possible. The dieting should also be stopped and gradually replaced by a normal eating pattern (three times a day and two snacks). You should gradually learn to discover that you can eat more, without putting on any weight. Remember that your hunger and satiation are disturbed and at first not reliable. Agreements should therefore be made upon times and quantities to eat.

Variety in food is also a necessity, as most diets are monotonous. Those ingredients of the food one would eat otherwise in binges (for instance, sweets), are then gradually incorporated into the meals by small quantities. This is a remedy to protect yourself against any new urge to overeat. The eating behavior should also be considered; for instance, learning to eat slowly by small bites, paying attention to the taste of the food. As to your weight, it is completely wrong to put oneself down to just one figure. It would be overlooking the natural fluctuations. It is better to determine a reasonable weight variation, that is, a minimum and a maximum limit, reckoning with body height, build, and age. It is best to weigh yourself only once a week, so as to avoid paying excessive attention to daily weight fluctuations.

The second phase of the treatment is aimed at the further stabilization of the eating pattern, on the one hand. On the other hand, more attention is now paid to the circumstances in which periods of overeating occur. Thoughts and feelings regarding nutrition, weight, and body shape are analyzed. We are searching for better means to abreact,

TABLE C-1.
Medical Complications

Periods of overeating	Self-induced vomiting	Laxative abuse
Sudden dilatation of the stomach with risk of rip in the stomach wall, menstrual disorders, painless swelling of salivary glands	Metabolic disorders (shortage of potassium), heart rhythm disorders, muscle spasms, general weakness, dehydration (drying up), epilepsy (falling sickness), renal damage	
	Dental decay, chronic hoarseness, sore throat,	Diarrhea, drumstick fingers

solve, or, even better, prevent possible tensions. A clear planning of activities and social contacts is very important in this respect.

The last phase of the guidance is aimed at further applying what you have learned in both previous phases, even when new difficulties occur. After all, conflicts and problems are to be expected in everybody's life. We attempt to find solutions to these challenges and to actually try them out. Eating problems may reemerge in periods of stress. You should regard your eating problems as a "weak spot": It is your way to respond whenever you are in trouble. Whenever you are inclined again to start overeating, it is usually caused by one or more unsolved difficulties or problems. You should therefore carefully consider what goes on in your life and what you are dissatisfied with. As soon as you know what it is all about, explore all possible solutions to these problems and draw a plan to solve them.

It remains important, however, to take timely steps to prevent a relapse into bulimia whenever you feel difficulties coming up:

1. Take time to reflect on your difficulties, to consider solutions, and to draw a plan for action. Some solutions help, others do not.

2. Start keeping a diary again concerning your eating habits.

3. Limit your eating to three planned meals and at most two snacks. Try to keep to stated times. As soon as you get the feeling of losing your control, plan your meals in detail (fixed portions stated beforehand).

4. Try as much as possible to be in the company of others, especially when eating.

5. Restrict your food supply. Whenever you feel that you are going to buy too much, take as little money as possible with you or plan your errands well in advance and look for company.

6. Plan your daily activities. Avoid both periods of "not knowing what to do" and those of "wanting to do everything at once."

7. Find out which moments give rise to overeating and plan activities that do not go with eating, such as looking up a friend, busying yourself with a hobby, etc.

8. Stay away from the kitchen or pantry between meals.

9. If you start brooding too much over your weight, impose the limitation of weighing yourself only once a week. If, however, it is necessary to lose weight, do so only after having normalized your eating habits again, and do it slowly and gradually by decreasing the quantities. In any case, do this rather than skipping meals. Remember, you must accept a weight variation. After all, it is only natural.

10. If you think too much about your figure, you may be feeling anxious or sad. You will probably have the feeling of being fat whenever something goes wrong. Try to detect the problems and to solve them, as well.

11. If possible, take someone into your confidence. Talk about your present difficulties. Remember, you wouldn't object to one of your friends talking about his or her problems to you.

12. Set limited objectives. It is often a question of trial and error. One "failure" is no evidence of a succession of failures. Also note your progress, however limited it may be.

Finally, look for support in time and remain honest with yourself.

References

Abraham, S. F., Mason, C., & Mira, M. (1985). Treatment of bulimia. In S. W. Touyz & P. J. V. Beumont (Eds.), *Eating disorders: Prevalence and treatment* (pp. 74–82). Sydney: William & Wilkins.

Agras, W. S., Schneider, J. A., Arnow, B., Raeburn, S. D., & Telch, C. (1989). Cognitive-behavioral and response-prevention treatments for bulimia nervosa. *Journal of Consulting and Clinical Psychology, 57*, 215–221.

American Psychiatric Association. (1980). *Diagnostic and statistical manual of mental disorders (3rd ed.)*. Washington, DC: Author.

American Psychiatric Association. (1987). *Diagnostic and statistical manual of mental disorders (3rd ed.-rev.)*. Washington, DC: Author.

Andersen, A. E. (1985). *Practical comprehensive treatment of anorexia nervosa and bulimia*. Baltimore: Johns Hopkins University Press.

Andersen, A. E. (Ed.) (1990). *Males with eating disorders*. New York: Brunner/Mazel.

Barabasz, M. (1990). Bulimia, hypnotizability and dissociative capacity. In R. Van Dyck, P. Spinhoven, A. J. W. Van der Does, Y. R. Van Rood, & W. De Moor (Eds.), *Hypnosis: Current theory, research and practice* (pp. 207–213). Amsterdam: V. U. Press.

Bemis, K. M. (1985). 'Abstinence' and 'nonabstinence' models for the treatment of bulimia. *International Journal of Eating Disorders, 4*, 407–438.

Birtchnell, S. A., Hart, A., & Lacey, J. H. (1986). Body image distortion in bulimia nervosa. In J. H. Lacey & D. A. Sturgeon (Eds.), *Proceedings of the 15th European conference on psychosomatic research* (pp. 148–152). London: John Libbey.

Brisman, J., & Siegel, M. (1985). The bulimia workshop: A unique integration of group treatment approaches. *International Journal of Group Psychotherapy, 35*, 585–601.

Cheek, D., & LeCron, L. (1968). Clinical hypnotherapy. New York: Grune & Stratton.

Cooper, W. J., & Fairburn, C. G. (1986). The depressive symptoms of bulimia nervosa. British Journal of Psychiatry, 143, 268.

Cox, G. L., & Meckel, W. T. (1989). A qualitative review of psychosocial treatments for bulimia. Journal of Nervous and Mental Disease, 177, 77–84.

Derogatis, L. R. (1977). The SCL-90. Baltimore: Clinical Psychometric Research.

Edelstein, M. G. (1982). Trauma, trance and transformation: A clinical guide to hypnotherapy. New York: Brunner/Mazel.

Fairburn, C. G. (1985). Cognitive-behavioral treatment for bulimia. In D. M. Garner & P. E. Garfinkel (Eds.), Handbook of psychotherapy for anorexia nervosa and bulimia (pp. 160–192). New York: Guilford Press.

Fairburn, C. G. (1987). The definition of bulimia nervosa: Guidelines for clinicians and research workers. Annals of Behavioral Medicine, 9, 3–7.

Fairburn, C. G. (1988). The current status of the psychological treatments for bulimia nervosa. Journal of Psychosomatic Research, 32, 635–645.

Fairburn, C. G., & Garner, D. M. (1986). The diagnosis of bulimia nervosa. International Journal of Eating Disorders, 5, 403–419.

Fairburn, C. G., Kirk, J., O'Connor, M., & Cooper, P. J. (1986). A comparison of two psychological treatments for bulimia nervosa. Behaviour Research and Therapy, 24, 629–643.

Fichter, M. M. (1992). The German longitudinal bulimia nervosa study. In W. Herzog, H. C. Deter, & W. Vandereycken (Eds.), The course of eating disorders: Long-term follow-up studies of anorexia and bulimia nervosa. Berlin-New York: Springer-Verlag.

Freeman, C. P. I., Barry, F., Dunkeld-Turnbull, J., & Henderson, A. (1988). Controlled trial of psychotherapy for bulimia nervosa. British Medical Journal, 296, 521–525.

Freeman, R. J., Thomas, C. D., Solyom, S., & Koopman, R. F. (1985). Clinical and personality correlates of body size overestimation in anorexia nervosa and bulimia nervosa. International Journal of Eating Disorders, 4, 439–456.

Garfinkel, P. E., & Garner, D. M. (Eds.) (1987). The role of drug treatments for eating disorders. New York: Brunner/Mazel.

Garner, D. M., & Fairburn, C. G. (1987). Cognitive-behavioral treatment of bulimia nervosa. Behavior Modification, 12, 398–431.

Garner, D. M., & Garfinkel, P. E. (Eds.) (1988). *Diagnostic issues in anorexia nervosa and bulimia nervosa*. New York: Brunner/Mazel.

Garner, D. M., Olmsted, M. P., & Polivy, J. (1983). Development and validation of a multidimensional eating disorder inventory for anorexia nervosa and bulimia. *International Journal of Eating Disorders, 2*(2), 15–33.

Garner, D. M., Rockert, W., Olmsted, M. G., Johnson, C., & Coscina, D. V. (1985). Psychoeducational principles in the treatment of bulimia and anorexia nervosa. In D. M. Garner & P. E. Garfinkel (Eds.), *Handbook of psychotherapy for anorexia nervosa and bulimia* (pp. 513–556). New York: Guilford Press.

Garner, D. M., Olmsted, M. P., Davis, R., Rockert, W., Goldbloom, D., & Eagle, M. (1990). The association between bulimic symptoms and reported psychopathology. *International Journal of Eating Disorders, 9*, 1–15.

Giles, R. T., Young, R. R., & Young, D. E. (1985). Behavioral treatment of severe bulimia. *Behavior Therapy, 16*, 393–405.

Glassman, J. N. S., Rich, C. L., Darko, D., & Clarkin, A. (1990). Some correlates of treatment response to a multicomponent psychotherapy program in outpatients with eating disorders. *Annals of Clinical Psychiatry, 2*, 33–38.

Goldbloom, D. S., Kennedy, S. H., Kaplan, A. S., & Woodside, D. B. (1989). Recent advances in pharmacotherapy: Anorexia nervosa and bulimia nervosa. *Canadian Medical Association Journal, 140*, 1149–1154.

Griffiths, R. A. (1990). Characteristics of dropouts and completers from hypnobehavioral treatment for bulimia nervosa. *International Journal of Eating Disorders, 9*, 217–219.

Hall, R. C. W., Tice, L., Beresford, T. P., Wooley, B., & Hall, A. K. (1989). Sexual abuse in patients with anorexia nervosa and bulimia. *Psychosomatics, 30*, 73–79.

Heilbrun, A. B., Bloomfield, J., & Bloomfield, D. L. (1986). Cognitive differences between bulimic and anorexic females: Self-control deficits in bulimia. *International Journal of Eating Disorders, 5*, 209–222.

Herzog, W., Deter, H. C., & Vandereycken, W. (Eds.). (1992). *The course of eating disorders: Long-term follow-up studies of anorexia and bulimia nervosa*. Berlin-New York: Springer-Verlag.

Hohlstein, L. A., Gwirtsman, H. E., Whalen, F., & Enns, M. P. (1986). Oral glucose tolerance in bulimia. *International Journal of Eating Disorders, 5*, 157–160.

Hsu, L. G. K. (1990). Experiential aspects of bulimia nervosa: Implications for cognitive behavioral therapy. *Behavior Modification, 14*, 50–65.

Hsu, L. G. K., & Holder, D. (1986). Bulimia nervosa: Treatment and short-term outcome. *Psychological Medicine, 16*, 65–70.

Hudson, J. I., & Pope, H. G. (1990). Psychopharmacological treatment of bulimia. In M. M. Fichter (Ed.), *Bulimia nervosa: Basic research, diagnosis, and therapy* (pp. 331–343). Chichester-New York: John Wiley.

Johnson, C., Tobin, D. L., & Dennis, D. (1990). Differences in treatment outcome between borderline and nonborderline bulimics at one-year follow-up. *International Journal of Eating Disorders, 9*, 617–627.

Johnson, W. G., Schlundt, D. G., & Jarell, M. P. (1986). Exposure with response prevention, training in energy balance and problem/solving therapy for bulimia nervosa. *International Journal of Eating Disorders, 5*, 35–46.

Kirkley, B. G., Schneider, J. A., Agras, W. S., & Bachman, J. A. (1985). Comparison of two group treatments, for bulimia. *Journal of Consulting and Clinical Psychology, 53*, 43–48.

Knapp, T. W. (1983). Verhaltenstherapie der Bulimia Nervosa/Bulimarexia: Eine kontrollierte Fallstudie. *Zeitschrift für Klinische Psychologie, 12*, 157–173.

Knight, J. C. & Litton, S. C. (1984). Psychological testing and eating disorders. In P. S. Powers & R. C. Fernandez (Eds.), *Current treatment of anorexia nervosa and bulimia* (pp. 241–264). Basel: Karger.

Krystal, P. (1982). *Cutting the ties that bind.* Columbus, Ohio: Turnstone Press.

Lacey, J. H. (1983). Bulimia nervosa, binge eating and vomiting: A controlled treatment study and long-term outcome. *British Medical Journal, 286*, 1609–1613.

Lacey, J. H. (1985). Time-limited individual and group treatment for bulimia. In D. M. Garner & P. E. Garfinkel (Eds.), *Handbook of psychotherapy for anorexia nervosa and bulimia* (pp. 431–457). New York: Guilford Press.

Lacey, J. H. (1986). Bulimia: Factors which influence treatment response. In J. H. Lacey & D. A. Sturgeon (Eds.), *Proceedings of the 15th European conference on psychosomatic research* (pp. 128–133). London: John Libbey.

Lacey, J. H. (1992). Long-term follow-up of bulimic patients treated in integrated behavioral and psychodynamic treatment programs. In W. Herzog, H. C. Deter, & W. Vandereycken (Eds.), *The course of eating disorders: Long-term follow-up studies of anorexia and bulimia nervosa.* Berlin-New York: Springer-Verlag.

Lacey, J. H., Cohen, S., & Birtchnell, S. A. (1986). Factors associated with the onset and maintenance of bulimia nervosa. In J. H. Lacey & D. A. Sturgeon (Eds.), *Proceedings of the 15th European conference on psychosomatic research* (pp. 142–147). London: John Libbey.

Laessle, R. G., Schweiger, U., Fichter, M. M., & Pirke, K. M. (1988). Eating disorders and depression: Psychobiological findings in bulimia and anorexia nervosa. In K. M. Pirke, W. Vandereycken, & D. Ploog (Eds.), *The psychobiology of bulimia nervosa* (pp. 90–100). Berlin-New York: Springer-Verlag.

Lange, A., & van der Hart, O. (1983). *Directive family therapy.* New York: Brunner/Mazel.

Leitenberg, H., & Rosen, J. (1989). Cognitive-behavioral therapy with and without exposure plus response-prevention in treatment of bulimia nervosa. *Journal of Consulting and Clinical Psychology, 57,* 776–777.

Leitenberg, H., Rosen, J. C., Gross, J., Nudelman, S., & Vara, L. S. (1988). Exposure plus response prevention treatment of bulimia nervosa. *Journal of Consulting and Clinical Psychology, 57,* 215–221.

Margittai, K. J., Blouin, A., & Pérez, E. (1987). A study of the dropouts in psychopharmacological research with bulimics. *International Journal of Psychiatry in Medicine, 16,* 297–304.

Merrill, C. A., Mines, R. A., & Starkey, R. (1987). The premature dropout in group treatment of bulimia. *International Journal of Eating Disorders, 6,* 293–300.

Minuchin, S., Rosman, B., & Baker, L. (1978). *Psychosomatic families: Anorexia nervosa in context.* Cambridge: Harvard University Press.

Mitchell, J. E., Davis, L., Goff, G., & Pyle, R. (1986). A follow-up study of patients with bulimia. *International Journal of Eating Disorders, 5,* 441–450.

Mitchell, J. E., Davis, L., & Gretchen, G. (1985a). The process of relapse in patients with bulimia. *International Journal of Eating Disorders, 4,* 457–463.

Mitchell, J. E., Hatsukami, D., Goff, G., Pyle, R. L., Eckert, E. E., & Davis, L. E. (1985b). Intensive outpatient group therapy for bulimia. In D. M. Garner & P. E. Garfinkel (Eds.), *Handbook of psychotherapy for anorexia nervosa and bulimia* (pp. 240–256). New York: Guilford Press.

Mitchell, J. E., & Pyle, R. L. (1992). A long-term follow-up study of outpatients with bulimia nervosa treated in a structured group psychotherapy program. In W. Herzog, H. C. Deter, & W. Vandereycken (Eds.),

The course of eating disorders: Long term follow-up studies of anorexia and bulimia nervosa. Berlin-New York: Springer-Verlag.

Mitchell, J. E., Pyle, R. L., Eckert, E. D., Hatsukami, D., Pomeroy, C., & Zimmerman, R. (1988). Preliminary results of a comparison treatment trial of bulimia nervosa. In K. M. Pirke, W. Vandereycken & D. Ploog (Eds.), *The psychobiology of bulimia nervosa* (pp. 152–157). Berlin-New York: Springer-Verlag.

Mitchell, P. B. (1988). The pharmacological management of bulimia nervosa: A critical review. *International Journal of Eating Disorders, 7*, 29–42.

Oesterheld, J. R., McKenna, M. S., & Gould, N. B. (1987). Group psychotherapy of bulimia: A critical review. *International Journal of Group Psychotherapy, 37*, 163–184.

Orbach, S. (1978). *Fat is a feminist issue.* London-New York: Paddington Press.

Ordman, A. M., & Kirschenbaum, D. S. (1985). Cognitive-behavioral therapy for bulimia: An initial outcome study. *Journal of Consulting and Clinical Psychology, 53*, 305–313.

Papp, P. (1983). *The process of change.* New York: Guilford Press.

Pettinati, H. M., Horne, R. J., & Staats, J. M. (1985). Hypnotizability in patients with anorexia nervosa and bulimia. *Archives of General Psychiatry, 42*, 1014–1016.

Piran, M., & Kaplan, A. S. (Eds.). (1990). *A day hospital group treatment program for anorexia nervosa and bulimia nervosa.* New York: Brunner/Mazel.

Polivy, J., & Herman, P. C. (1985). Dieting and bingeing. *American Psychologist, 40*, 193–201.

Pope, H., & Hudson, J. (1985). Biological treatment of eating disorders. In S. W. Emmett (Ed.), *Theory and treatment of anorexia nervosa and bulimia* (pp. 73–92). New York: Brunner/Mazel.

Pyle, M. L., Mitchell, J. E., Eckert, E. D., Hatsukami, D., Pomeroy, C., & Zimmerman, M. (1990). Maintenance treatment and 6-months outcome for bulimic patients who respond to initial treatment. *American Journal of Psychiatry, 147*, 871–875.

Root, M. P., & Fallon, P. (1989). Treating the victimized bulimic: The functions of binge-purge behavior. *Journal of Interpersonal Violence, 4*, 90–100.

Root, M. P., Fallon, P., & Friedrich, N. W. (1986). *Bulimia: A systems approach to treatment.* New York: W. W. Norton.

Rosen, J. C. (1987). A review of behavioral treatments for bulimia nervosa. *Behavior Modification, 12*, 464–486.

Rosen, J. C., & Leitenberg, H. (1988). The anxiety model of bulimia nervosa and treatment with exposure plus response prevention. In K. M. Pirke, W. Vandereycken, & D. Ploog (Eds.), *The psychobiology of bulimia nervosa* (pp. 146–151). Berlin-New York: Springer-Verlag.

Russell, G. F. M. (1979). Bulimia nervosa: An ominous variant of anorexia nervosa. *Psychological Medicine, 9*, 429–448.

Russell, G. F., Smukler, G. I., Dare, C., & Eisler, I. (1987). An evaluation of family therapy in anorexia nervosa and bulimia nervosa. *Archives of General Psychiatry, 44*, 1047–1050.

Sanders, S. (1986). The perceptual alteration scale: A scale measuring dissociation. *American Journal of Clinical Hypnosis, 29*, 95–102.

Schechter, I. D., Schwartz, H. P., & Greenfeld, D. G. (1987). Sexual assault and anorexia nervosa. *International Journal of Eating Disorders, 6*, 313–316.

Schneider, J. A., & Agras, W. S. (1985). A cognitive behavioral group treatment of bulimia. *British Journal of Psychiatry, 146*, 66–69.

Schwartz, R. C., Barrett, M. J., & Saba, G. (1985). Family therapy for bulimia. In D. M. Garner & P. E. Garfinkel (Eds.), *Handbook of psychotherapy for anorexia nervosa and bulimia* (pp. 280–310). New York: Guilford Press.

Sloan, G., & Leichner, P. (1986). Is there a relationship between sexual abuse or incest and eating disorders? *Canadian Journal of Psychiatry, 31*, 656–660.

Steinberg, S., Tobin, D., & Johnson, C. (1990). The role of bulimic behaviors in affect regulation: Different functions for different patient subgroups. *International Journal of Eating Disorders, 9*, 51–55.

Thompson, D. A., Berg, K. M., & Shatford, L. A. (1987). The heterogeneity of bulimic symptomatology: Cognitive and behavioral dimensions. *International Journal of Eating Disorders, 6*, 125–137.

Torem, M. S. (1986a). Eating disorders and dissociative states. In F. E. F. Larocca (Ed.), *Eating disorders: Effective care and treatment* (pp. 141–150). St. Louis: Ishiyaku EuroAmerica.

Torem, M. S. (1986b). Dissociative states presenting as an eating disorder. *American Journal of Clinical Hypnosis, 29*, 137–142.

Torem, M. S. (1987). Ego state therapy for eating disorders. *American Journal of Clinical Hypnosis, 38*, 101–111.

Van Coppenolle, H., Probst, M., Vandereycken, W., Goris, M., & Meermann, R. (1990). Construction of a questionnaire on the body experience of anorexia nervosa. In H. Remschmidt & M. H. Schmidt

(Eds.), *Anorexia nervosa* (pp. 103–113). Toronto-Bern-Stuttgart: Hogrefe & Huber.

Vandereycken, W. (1985). Inpatient treatment of anorexia nervosa: Some research-guided changes. *Journal of Psychiatric Research, 19,* 413–422.

Vandereycken, W. (1987a). Are anorexia nervosa and bulimia variants of affective disorder? *Acta Psychiatrica Belgica, 87,* 267–280.

Vandereycken, W. (1987b). The constructive family approach to eating disorders: Critical remarks on the use of family therapy in anorexia nervosa and bulimia. *International Journal of Eating Disorders, 6,* 455–467.

Vandereycken, W. (1987c). The management of patients with anorexia nervosa and bulimia: Basic principles and general guidelines. In P. J. V. Beumont, G. D. Burrows, & R. C. Casper (Eds.), *Handbook of eating disorders: Vol. 1. Anorexia and bulimia nervosa* (pp. 235–253). Amsterdam: Elsevier-North Holland.

Vandereycken, W. (1988). Organization and evaluation of an inpatient treatment program for eating disorders. *Behavioral Residential Treatment, 3,* 153–165.

Vandereycken, W. (1990a). The addiction model in eating disorders. *International Journal of Eating Disorders, 9,* 95–101.

Vandereycken, W. (1990b). The relevance of body image disturbances for the treatment of bulimia. In M. M. Fichter (Ed.), *Bulimia nervosa: Basic research, diagnosis and treatment* (pp. 320–330). Chichester-New York: John Wiley.

Vandereycken, W., Kog, E., & Vanderlinden, J. (1989). *The family approach to eating disorders: Assessment and treatment of anorexia nervosa and bulimia.* New York/Costa Mesa, CA: PMA Publications.

Vandereycken, W., & Meermann, R. (1984). *Anorexia nervosa: A clinician's guide to treatment.* Berlin-New York: Walter de Gruyter.

Vandereycken, W., & Vanderlinden, J. (1983). Denial of illness and the use of self-reporting measures in anorexia nervosa patients. *International Journal of Eating Disorders, 2*(4), 101–107.

Vandereycken, W., Vanderlinden, J., & Van Werde, D. (1986). Directive group therapy for patients with anorexia nervosa or bulimia. In F. E. F. Larocca (Ed.), *Eating disorders: Effective care and treatment* (pp. 53–69). St. Louis: Ishiyaku EuroAmerica.

Vanderlinden, J., & Vandereycken, W. (1987). The effect of a residential treatment program in eating disorder patients and their families. In W.

Huber (Ed.), *Progress in psychotherapy research* (pp. 407–420). Louvain-La Neuve: Presses Universitaires de Louvain.

Vanderlinden, J., & Vandereycken, W. (1988a). Family therapy in bulimia nervosa. In D. Hardoff & E. Chigier (Eds.), *Eating disorders in adolescents and young adults* (pp. 325–334). London: Freund Publishing House.

Vanderlinden, J., & Vandereycken, W. (1988b). Perception of changes in eating disorder patients during group treatment. *Psychotherapy and Psychosomatics, 49,* 160–163.

Vanderlinden, J., & Vandereycken, W. (1988c). The use of hypnotherapy in the treatment of eating disorders. *International Journal of Eating Disorders, 7,* 673–679.

Vanderlinden, J., & Vandereycken, W. (1989). The place of family therapy in the treatment of chronic eating disorders. *Journal of Strategic and Systemic Therapies, 8*(1), 18–23.

Vanderlinden, J., & Vandereycken, W. (1990). The use of hypnosis in the treatment of bulimia nervosa. *International Journal of Clinical and Experimental Hypnosis, 38,* 101–111.

Vanderlinden, J., Van Dyck, R., & Vandereycken, W. (1990). *Hypnotizability and dissociation in eating disorders.* Paper presented at the 5th European Congress of Hypnosis, Konstanz, Germany.

Watkins, S. (1971). The affect bridge: A hypnoanalytic technique. *International Journal of Clinical and Experimental Hypnosis, 19,* 21–27.

Watkins, J. G., & Watkins, H. H. (1982). Ego state therapy. In L. E. Abt & L. R. Stuart (Eds.), *The newer therapies: A sourcebook* (pp. 136–155). New York: Van Nostrand Reinhold.

Weiss, L., Katzman, M. A., & Wolchik, S. A. (1985). *Treating bulimia: A psycho-educational approach.* New York-Oxford: Pergamon Press.

Wertheim, L. H. (1988). Predictors of response to a group therapy program for bulimics. In D. Hardoff & E. Chigier (Eds.), *Eating disorders in adolescents and young adults* (pp. 335–348). London: Freund Publishing House.

White, W. C., & Boskind-Lodahl, M. (1981). An experiential-behavioral approach to the treatment of bulimarexia. *Psychotherapy: Theory, Research, and Practice, 18,* 501–507.

Wilmuth, M. E. H., Leitenberg, H., Rosen, J. C., Fondacaro, K. M., & Gross, J. (1985). Body size distortion in bulimia nervosa. *International Journal of Eating Disorders, 4,* 71–78.

Wilson, G. T. (1986). Cognitive-behavioral and pharmacological therapies for bulimia. In K. D. Brownell & J. P. Foreyt (Eds.), *Handbook of eating disorders* (pp. 450–475). New York: Basic Books.

Wilson, G. T. (1989). The treatment of bulimia nervosa: A cognitive-social learning analysis. In A. J. Stunkard & A. Baum (Eds.), *Perspectives in behavioral medicine: Eating, sleeping and sex* (pp. 73–98). Hillsdale, NJ: Lawrence Erlbaum Associates.

Wilson, G. T., Rossiter, E., Kliefield, E. I., & Lindholm, L. (1986). Cognitive-behavioral treatment of bulimia nervosa: A controlled evaluation. *Behaviour Research and Therapy, 24,* 277–288.

Wonderlich, S. A., & Smitt, W. J. (1990). Borderline versus other personality disorders in the eating disorders: Clinical description. *International Journal of Eating Disorders, 9,* 629–638.

Wonderlich, S. A., Smitt, W. J., Slotnick, W. B., & Goodman, S. (1990). DSM-III-R personality disorders in eating disorder subtypes. *International Journal of Eating Disorders, 9,* 807–816.

Wooley, S.C., & Kearny-Cooke, A. (1986). Intensive treatment of bulimia and body-image disturbance. In K. D. Brownell & J. P. Foreyt (Eds.), *Handbook of eating disorders* (pp. 476–502). New York: Basic Books.

Wooley, S. C., & Wooley, O. W. (1985). Intensive outpatient and residential treatment for bulimia. In D. M. Garner & P. E. Garfinkel (Eds.), *Handbook of psychotherapy for anorexia nervosa and bulimia* (pp. 391–430). New York: Guilford Press.

Wright, M. E., & Wright, B. A. (1982). *Clinical practice of hypnotherapy.* New York: Guilford Press.

Yager, J. (1985). The outpatient treatment of bulimia. *Bulletin of the Menninger Clinic, 49,* 203–226.

Name Index

Subject Index